COMBAT ARMS

MODERN ATTACK

AIRCRAFT

BILL GUNSTON

Published by Salamander Books Limited
LONDON • NEW YORK

A Salamander Book

Published by
Salamander Books Ltd.,
52 Bedford Row,
London WC1R 4LR,
United Kingdom.

©Salamander Books Ltd. 1989

ISBN 0 86101 451 0

Distributed in the United Kingdom by
Hodder & Stoughton Services
PO Box 6, Mill Road
Dunton Green, Sevenoaks,
Kent TN13 2XX.

All rights reserved. No part of this book
may be reproduced, stored in a retrieval system
or transmitted in any form or by any means
electronic, mechanical, recording or otherwise,
without the prior permission
of Salamander Books Ltd.

All correspondence concerning the content of
this volume should be addressed to the publisher.

Credits

Editor: Lindsay Peacock
Designer: Rod Ferring
Colour artwork: Terry Hadler, Michael Keep and
Stephen Seymour (©Salamander Books Ltd.).
Filmset by The Old Mill
Colour reproduction by Kentscan
Printed in Belgium by Proost International
Book Production, Turnhout.

The Author

Bill Gunston is a former RAF pilot and flying instructor. He has acted as advisor to several aviation companies and has become one of the most internationally respected authors and broadcasters on aviation and scientific subjects. He is author of numerous books on aviation and other military subjects, is a regular contributor to many international defence periodicals, is Assistant Compiler of *Jane's All The World's Aircraft* and was responsible for the companion volume entitled *Modern Fighters*.

Contents

Introduction	6
Aeritalia/Aermacchi/EMBRAER AMX	16
Aermacchi M.B.339	18
BAe Buccaneer	20
BAe Harrier and Sea Harrier	22
BAe Hawk	24
BAe Strikemaster	26
Cessna T-37 and A-37B Dragonfly	28
Dassault-Breguet Mirage 5	30
Dassault-Breguet Super Etendard	32
Dassault-Dornier Alpha Jet	34
Fairchild Republic A-10A Thunderbolt II	36
FMA IA 58 and IA 66 Pucara	38
General Dynamics F-111	40
Grumman A-6 Intruder	42
IAR/Soko Orao	44
Lockheed F-117A	46
McDonnell Douglas A-4 Skyhawk	48
McDonnell Douglas F-4 Phantom II	50
McDonnell Douglas F-18 Hornet	52
McDonnell Douglas/BAe AV-8B/Harrier II	54
MiG-23/27 (Flogger)	56
Mitsubishi F-1 and T-2	58
NAMC Q-5 (Fantan)	60
Panavia Tornado IDS	60
Saab 37 Viggen	64
SEPECAT Jaguar	66
Su-17/20/22 (Fitter)	68
Su-24 (Fencer)	70
Su-25 (Frogfoot)	72
Vought (LTV) A-7 Corsair II	74
XAC H-7	76
Index	78

MODERN ATTACK AIRCRAFT

ATTACK TECHNOLOGY

UNTIL THE 1960s, attacks from the air on surface targets could be carried out by two chief classes of warplane: bombers and attack aircraft. The bomber carried a bomb aimer or bombardier who could take careful aim on the target with a precision sight, the aircraft flying straight and level at medium to high altitude. The attack aircraft had none of these things and might well be a single-seater, so the only way it could attack was either in a shallow dive, for firing guns or rockets or dropping bombs according to the pilot's judgement, or in a very steep (ideally vertical) dive from which a bomb could be released with a fair degree of precision.

It will be self-evident that the attack aircraft's capabilities were sharply reduced, if not eliminated, at night or in conditions of very poor visibility. Likewise, the capabilities of the bomber had to be re-thought in the early 1960s when it was reluctantly realised that SAMs (surface-to-air missiles), and even enemy fighters, would be likely to shoot down 100 per cent of the raiding force. The only answer for all aircraft attempting to penetrate defended airspace was to fly at the lowest possible safe height, in order to try to stay in the region close to the ground below the lowest probing "lobes" of the defending radars. Of course, to every weapon and counter-weapon there is always an answer, and today "look-down" radars sited on hills or towers, or carried in the noses of enemy fighters, can pick out air targets moving at speed across the terrain or sea just beneath. Despite this, as described in the section on Missions and Tactics, low level (or Lo) is still regarded as being much safer for non-stealth aircraft than any other flight level.

To fly at low level made new demands on the technology. Some effects are obvious. The aircraft, with or possibly without the help of its crew, had to be able to navigate with the Earth's surface rushing past as a blur close underneath, and with no opportunity to climb to get a good overall view of the terrain or — and this was serious — the target. Means had to be provided to avoid hitting the ground and this eventually required the development of wholly automatic systems called "terrain following" or "terrain avoidance" which were so reliable that the safety of the aircraft and its crew could be entrusted to them 100 per cent. New forms of sighting, ranging and weapon delivery had to be devised, even with the target dead ahead, approaching at perhaps 800 knots (902mph) and not seen until the last moments before weapon release. Not least, the aircraft had to give the crew a feeling of confidence and a ride quality through dense and often turbulent air that was always smooth enough for them to maintain their mental and physical faculties.

Traditional bombers could use radars to create electronic maps of the terrain below, seen from a steep look-down angle, and special doppler radars to give a read-out of exact groundspeed and drift. At very low level, however, neither of these desirable things is possible. Radars, lasers or IR devices have to look out ahead or sideways at an almost horizontal angle. It is still possible, but difficult, to obtain a clear ground map on our radar display. As we cannot "see" far with a low-level radar, we have to use a very short range display, which in turn means both that we see only a small distance ahead and the display moves very fast. Moreover, we can encounter problems caused by the fact that the terrain — hills, trees and other objects — can hem us in, so that, as

Above: Tradesmen of the Royal Air Force hold the antenna of the Tornado GR.1's attack radar during routine servicing. Visible just below it is the smaller dish associated with the terrain-following radar.

we thread our way along a helpfully screening valley, our sensors have hardly any vision except ahead. Really, we want at least one sensor, preferably the main radar, to look out to each side to give us what are called doppler velocities, by measuring the exact speed and direction of each spot of ground that our radar beam falls on. Only by this means can we update our INS (inertial navigation system), which, because it is self-contained, is the primary navigation method in almost all modern attack aircraft.

Before looking again at the main radar and other sensors, we must note the crucial importance of the TFR (terrain-following radar) or TAR (avoidance), which are essential for safe flight at high speed and low level, even on a clear day when the pilot can see ahead. When making a terrain-following attack through cloud-covered mountains, the need for absolute trust in the electronics is obvious! There are various definitions, but in general a TFR looks dead ahead while a TAR frequently interrupts the forward-looking scan to give a quick sweep to right and left. Thus, a TAR helps in defining the best course to follow along a winding valley.

Introduction

Both types of radar are linked via digital data buses to the automatic flight control system and thence to power units which drive the control surfaces. There always has to be some kind of monitoring circuit or, alternatively, three or four parallel electronic channels, so that any failure can be either over-ridden by those remaining or else identified as a fault and bypassed. If there are repeated failures, there eventually would come a time when automatic terrain following is no longer possible, and then a special signal warns the pilot and automatically pulls the aircraft up into a climb to a height at which he can safely take control.

One of the inescapable problems of high speed flight at low level is the violent buffeting experienced as the aircraft flies through the dense turbulent air. This exerts a powerful influence on the basic design of the aircraft, as explained in the next section. A very few aircraft, including the B-1B, are equipped with active flight control systems to minimise turbulence, which can have serious effects. In the B-1B, the SMCS (structural mode control system) is commanded by a set of sensitive accelerometers in the fuselage. Throughout each mission, these detect lateral (side to side) and vertical accelerations, such as are caused by flight through turbulent air. Their output signals are passed through a computer and then used to command the hydraulic power units driving two delta (triangular) control surfaces which slope down on each side of the forward fuselage. These surfaces, resembling small tailplanes, can work either together, to cancel out vertical accelerations, or in opposite directions, to cancel out lateral motions. As a result, the B-1B can fly through rough air at full throttle without either suffering fatigue damage or the crew "having their eyeballs shaken out". Small tactical attack aircraft cannot have such equipment.

Every attack aircraft has to have some form of advanced sighting and weapon-aiming system. Almost always, the sight takes the form of a HUD (head-up display), which comprises one or more boxes of electronics and a very flat and accurate pane of glass arranged directly in front of the pilot's eyes near the windscreen and sloping back (roughly parallel to the windscreen) at about 45°. The pilot can look straight through the screen and see everything coming up ahead, but he can also see on the screen — which is focussed at infinity so that he does not have to adjust his eyesight — various bright lines, numbers and symbols. These are generated by the electronics and provide steering guidance for navigation, weapon aiming and, often, for bad-weather landing. All HUDs can generate cursive symbols formed from strokes or lines (printed letters or symbols, or handwriting, are cursive), while a few can also generate a raster display made up of numerous closely spaced lines (a TV is a raster display). A raster display enables the HUD to show the pilot a complete picture of the scene ahead generated by a radar or FLIR (forward-looking infra-red).

Modern HUDs can be switched to any one of three modes: cruise, surface (or ground) attack and air combat (or air-to-air). In the cruise mode, the HUD displays such data as speed, height, heading, range, time to next waypoint or destination, Mach, vertical velocity and acceleration (g). In the surface attack mode, the display shows such things as CCIP (continuously computed impact point) or CCRP (release point) and, sometimes, aiming symbols for toss bombing or the level laydown release of retarded bombs (described in the

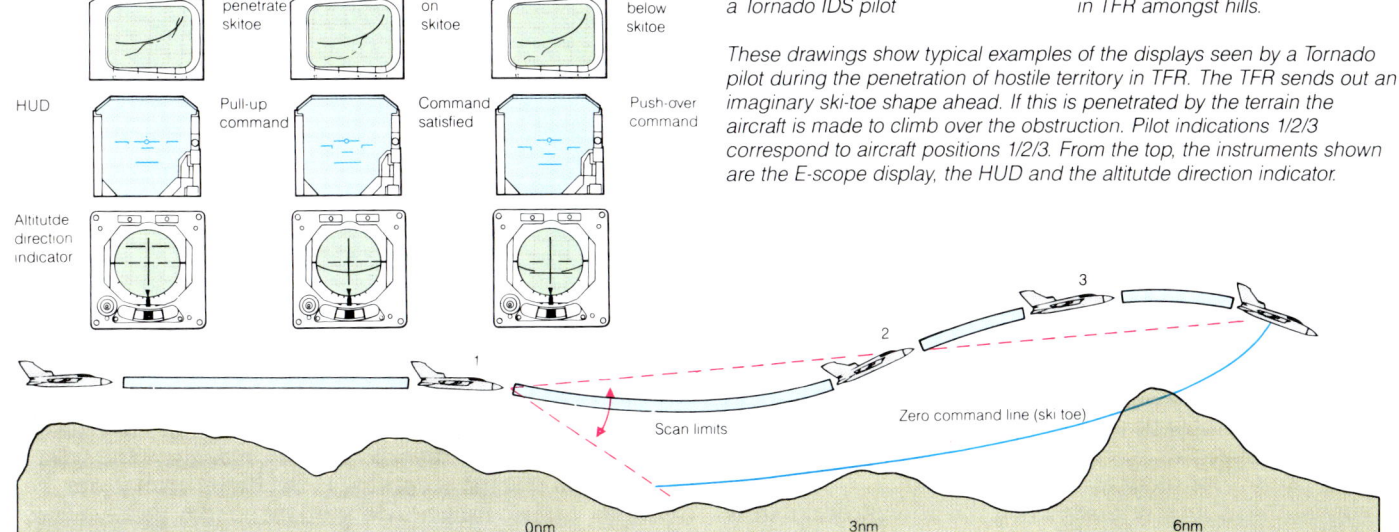

Left: Simplified displays as seen by a Tornado IDS pilot.

Foot of page: Tornado flight profile in TFR amongst hills.

These drawings show typical examples of the displays seen by a Tornado pilot during the penetration of hostile territory in TFR. The TFR sends out an imaginary ski-toe shape ahead. If this is penetrated by the terrain the aircraft is made to climb over the obstruction. Pilot indications 1/2/3 correspond to aircraft positions 1/2/3. From the top, the instruments shown are the E-scope display, the HUD and the altitutde direction indicator.

MODERN ATTACK AIRCRAFT

Above: The British Aerospace/McDonnell Douglas AV-8B Harrier II, now well established in service with the US Marine Corps and the Royal Air Force, combines clear cockpit displays with a good forward field of view.

Above: Carried by the General Dynamics F-111F, Pave Tack is an attack aid combining forward-looking infra red and laser sensors. Despite its great bulk and weight, it is nevertheless a worthwhile piece of kit.

section on Weapons). In the air combat mode, the HUD will provide aiming symbology for smooth tracking or snap-shooting with a gun and cueing or aiming/range markers for different types of missile.

Advanced HUDs incorporating raster pictures have to be linked with a forward-looking sensor such as a radar, FLIR or laser. All of these are basically similar, differing in their wavelength. Radars typically work with wavelengths of about 2 or 3cm; FLIRs and lasers typically use infra-red radiation with a wavelength of about one-ten-thousandth of a millimetre, or about 300,000 times shorter than radars. Such very short waves can generate much sharper pictures than radars and measure target range far more accurately, but they are more rapidly attenuated by cloud, rain, fog or smoke. All these sensors can play a major role in enabling the pilot to see ahead under adverse conditions, measure the range to targets accurately and guide weapons. Thus, they are essential for any aircraft that wishes to operate at night or in bad weather and it must be emphasised that any attack aircraft that can operate only in clear daytime visual conditions is utterly useless for modern warfare.

One of the problems confronting the aircraft designer is how far such devices should be built-in and how far they should be carried in one or more external pods. The same is true of EW (electronic warfare) devices, such as passive warning receivers and active jammers. Passive receivers use antennas on the tail or wingtips, and sometimes above or below the fuselage, to warn if the aircraft is being tracked by a hostile radar or laser. In advanced versions, they may also identify the kind of emitter being used and its direction. Active jammers transmit high-power noise on the same wavelengths as the enemy radar to spoil the picture seen by the enemy. Other countermeasures include chaff, which consists of billions of fine slivers of metallised foil to fill the sky with radar reflectors behind which our own aircraft can hide, and IRCM (infra-red countermeasures) of which the most common are high-power pulsed heat lamps and bright flares ejected from cylinders like large shotgun cartridges.

Modern attack aircraft are equipped with a central EW and countermeasures management system. This ensures that all the time that the aircraft is in hostile airspace, its passive receiver systems are ceaselessly "listening" for enemy emissions. When it detects any, the management system grades them in a list according to the threat each poses. For example, a close-range SAM guidance radar poses a more immediate threat than a long-range surveillance radar. The system then automatically decides what action to take and switches on particular jamming wavelengths or fires particular chaff cartridges, without the pilot having to do more than note what is happening.

Even today, the Tornado IDS normally goes into action with both outer-wing pylons occupied by defensive payloads, such as a chaff/flare dispenser on one and a jammer pod on the other. This aircraft was planned in the 1960s when customer air forces did not want integral defensive systems, thinking that they would constitute a weight and bulk penalty that often would not be needed. Today, it is impossible to imagine a war scenario in which such systems would not be of crucial importance, so today's combat aircraft are in the main now designed with internal defensive systems.

AIRCRAFT DESIGN

THE OVERALL category of Attack Aircraft today includes small turboprops and even piston-engined trainers, but this book concentrates on the jets, which are the only types most people would consider had a realistic chance of penetrating airspace defended by modern weapons. Most of these aircraft look like the popular idea of a fighter and would probably be described as fighters by the popular media; but the term "fighter" means an aircraft whose purpose is the destruction of enemy aircraft in the air. Many of the aircraft in this book are totally unable to do this.

For example, the Buccaneer, one of the most effective attack aircraft and loved by its crews, has neither the avionics, nor the agility nor the weapons to shoot down enemy aircraft. On the other hand, the F/A-18 is a true dual-role aircraft, able to fly either attack or fighter missions; but this means that, to varying degrees, it is penalized in not being quite right for either mission. This extends, for example, to the shape of the wing, but this is mainly a matter of structure and aerodynamics and is thus discussed later under that heading. For the moment, it is interesting to list the types examined in this book and outline what sort of aircraft they are. It can be seen that hardly any two are alike.

From the viewpoint of propulsion, the Argentinian Pucará is clearly the odd man out. It was originally designed to quell internal rebels with small arms and similar limited-war weapons. Thus, it was required to operate from short unpaved airstrips, to carry a fair amount of firepower over quite long ranges, to have good endurance at low level, but not to break the sound barrier. Two turboprops was a sensible choice, just as it was in the case of an American Co-In (counter-insurgency) aircraft, the Rockwell OV-10 Bronco. Such aircraft were not designed to come up against forces equipped with modern weapons. In the fighting in the Falklands in 1982,

the 24 Pucarás involved had no influence on the campaign and all were lost. This in no way invalidates the design, which was for a different purpose.

To some degree, the choice of engine is dictated by mission requirements, by national capabilities, by price and by customer preference in such matters as whether or not two engines are better than one. There is now evidence from millions of hours of operation in thousands of combat aircraft around the world, and the author challenges anyone to draw from it the conclusion that two engines make combat aircraft safer, or suffer a lower rate of attrition. On the other hand, the attack mission is the one most likely to suffer from birdstrikes, so — in the face of the numerical evidence — two engines ought to be better than one. In any case, there are secondary reaons for preferring two engines. For example, if the Su-24 were single-engined, the resulting power unit would be huge and unwieldy, and it would be more difficult to provide the necessary duplication of secondary power systems.

This aircraft (the Su-24) is believed to be powered by turbojets and this is surprising because it is quite a modern design, conceived well into the era in which it was appreciated that, even for supersonic aircraft, the turbofan can be more efficient than the turbojet, and burn less fuel. Moreover, for a supersonic aircraft with augmentation (burning extra fuel in the bypass air and a jetpipe afterburner),

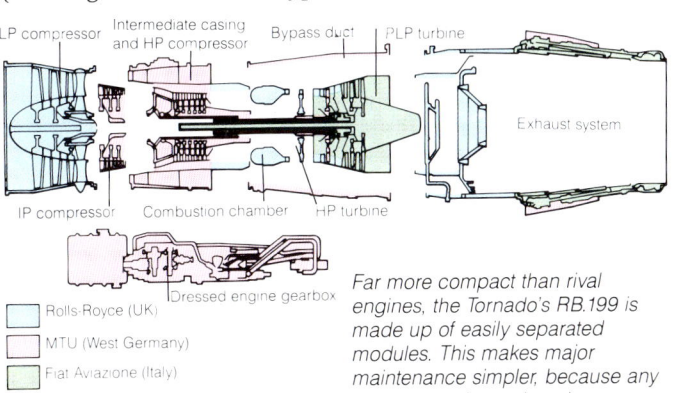

Far more compact than rival engines, the Tornado's RB.199 is made up of easily separated modules. This makes major maintenance simpler, because any module can be replaced.

the thrust of a turbofan can be boosted more than that of a turbojet because of the high proportion of available oxygen in the bypass airflow. For example, the extremely compact RB.199 engine which powers the Tornado has an augmentation thrust boost of about 77 per cent. Such a figure is difficult to achieve with a turbojet; the afterburner of the engine installed in the Su-17 family, and thought to be fitted to the Su-24, gives a boost of only 37 per cent. The Su-25 is known to have a simple turbojet, whereas the engine of the equivalent Western aircraft, the A-10A, is a highly efficient

MODERN ATTACK AIRCRAFT

turbofan burning much less fuel (and, incidentally, putting out much less noise and IR radiation). If the long-range Su-24 really does prove to have turbojet engines, it will merely underscore the Soviet emphasis on toughness and the use of long-proven hardware, rather than new engines burning less fuel.

Except for one or two dedicated anti-tank aircraft, there were very few specialised attack aircraft until about 1960. Attack missions were traditionally flown by fighters, especially by fighters that were either second-rate or slightly obsolescent. The only exception to this rule was found in naval aircraft. Britain favoured strange aircraft called "torpedo fighters" which were too small and short-ranged to fly useful torpedo missions and were far too big and clumsy to have any success as fighters. The US Navy alone had a long history of dedicated attack aircraft, of which three of Ed Heinemann's designs are among the most famous: the A-1 Skyraider, with a single big piston engine; the A-3 Skywarrior, a large long-range attacker with two jets; and the A-4 Skyhawk, with a single jet. These were successful because they did not also pretend to be fighters.

The Skywarrior was one of the few naval attack aircraft designed with a large internal weapons bay and no external weapon pylons. Another is the Buccaneer, which was also designed with four wing hardpoints. The beauty of the Buccaneer's internal bay is that it can be equipped to carry either a heavy bomb load or reconnaissance sensors, whilst the rotating door serves as a fuel tank. With an internal bomb load of 4,000lb (1,814kg), the "Bucc" is faster at sea level than a Mirage or Phantom with the same bomb load and burns very much less fuel because it needs no afterburners. Today, it is very much the exception. Almost across the board, attack aircraft hang all their bombs, missiles, tanks and jammer pods on the outside, along with any self-defence AAMs they may carry. Not only does this increase drag but it also greatly augments the RCS (radar cross-section), making the aircraft easier to detect at a distance. Aircraft manufacturers almost never publish figures for the performance of their attack aircraft carrying a representative weapon load and certainly not when carrying the maximum load. A careful check through *Jane's* suggests that in every case the maximum speed (no matter what height) is for the "clean" aircraft, though the Chinese do supply the take-off speed or run for the Q-5 with maximum weapon load! This is unhelpful, because not one of these aircraft could ever fly a combat mission in the "clean" condition.

Today, air staffs and manufacturers around the world are very slowly realising that there is something called LO (low observables) or stealth. Most are not doing much about it, apart from to wish they had the money to stay competitive. A few are paying lip-service to the new technology by tinkering with design details and putting something in their brochures about "radar absorbent coatings". Those who can, such as the big names in the United States, are actually building LO aircraft. The first include the F-117A, B-2 and A-12 (ATA, Advanced Tactical Aircraft). The YF-22 and YF-23 (ATF, Advanced Tactical Fighters) are also certain to be very strongly influenced by LO technology. One obvious feature of such aircraft will be totally internal weapon carriage, while the semi-LO designs will use conformal carriage. These matters are discussed later.

MISSIONS AND TACTICS

CLEARLY, the way the mission is flown depends chiefly on the nature of the target, its defences and the weapons to be used against it. It could also be influenced by the aircraft employed, but this has not often been a major factor.

This book is concerned with attack aircraft used mainly against tactical targets on land or sea. No sensible high command would use such aircraft to attack fixed targets, such

Below: The British Aerospace Alarm (Air-Launched Anti-Radiation Missile) will revolutionize missions.

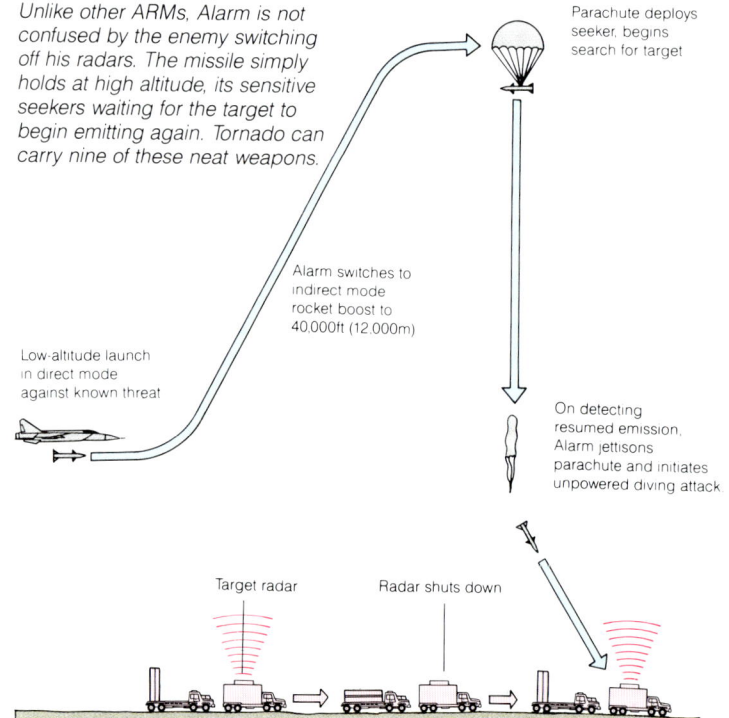

Unlike other ARMs, Alarm is not confused by the enemy switching off his radars. The missile simply holds at high altitude, its sensitive seekers waiting for the target to begin emitting again. Tornado can carry nine of these neat weapons.

Introduction

as factories or airfields, because such installations can be wiped out far more effectively by missiles. Such missiles are deployed by most major powers, with the notable exception of Britain. Having in 1957 been the only country to "go overboard" on missiles to an obviously ludicrous degree, stating that development of all future fighters, bombers and attack aircraft would be stopped (their place being taken by missiles), Britain was then the only country to fail to arm itself with any tactical missiles whatsoever, apart from a dozen launchers for the small short-range American Lance.

Be that as it may, the existence of high-precision missiles, with a CEP (circular error probability) in the order of 10m (33ft) and various kinds of nuclear, chemical, incendiary, binary, submunition or fuel/air explosive warhead, exerts a profound influence on the missions flown by tactical attack aircraft. Aircraft will be needed at least throughout the remainder of this century to attack moving armies and hostile fleets, though missiles exist which, having been fired into the known general area of such targets, can look down from above, detect and select targets and home on them automatically. Even quite small weapons now have this capability.

Thus, our tactical aircraft are going to be needed to destroy especially difficult, very fast or highly mobile targets and, occasionally, pinpoint targets where it is judged that a human crew would stand a better chance of differentiating between real targets and dummies and decoys (though if an area has been properly mapped and is subject to satellite scrutiny no missile with a modern guidance system could fail to pick the correct target location). Certainly, today's amazing interest by air forces and weapon manufacturers in devices intended to be dropped by manned aircraft on airfields must eventually be seen to be nonsensical.

It has already been explained that, unless the enemy's anti-aircraft defences are almost non-existent, it is prudent to fly through his airspace at the lowest possible level, commensurate with the wish to avoid overstressing the aircraft or hitting the ground. The abbreviation Lo is often used for such an attack profile (as distinct from Hi, which typically means 35,000ft or thereabouts, where a supersonic aircraft can reach its maximum speed), but with the emergence of LO as the acronym for "low observables" this can lead to confusion. What is meant by a low profile varies. In training, 500ft (150m) above the terrain is not an uncommon clearance, but in warfare pilots would invariably come down to 200ft (60m). RAF pilots and a few others are prepared to maintain 100ft (30m), but the actual clearance depends on the terrain and the groundspeed. In general, the faster the aircraft and the more irregular the terrain, the greater the clearance has to be.

The latest nav/attack avionic systems can automatically select a "best route" through defended territory, not only avoiding the defence installations previously stored in the computer memory but also those detected and identified a split second beforehand as the mission proceeds. Most air forces faced with a sophisticated enemy would never send attack aircraft on dangerous missions without some form of back-up. The two chief back-up aircraft categories are EW and SEAD.

EW (electronic warfare) plays a central role in almost every mission on land, sea or air undertaken "in the face of the enemy". In the case of attack aircraft, it is desirable to detect, identify and neutralise every enemy defence system that is encountered, but it is a tall order to do this and still carry a worthwhile ordnance load to the target.

It helps if a raiding force can have the support of dedicated EW aircraft such as the EF-111A Raven. These can precede the attacking aircraft, detecting, jamming and seeding with chaff or flares. They can, if necessary, fly with the attacking force or they can stand off in various ways to create a barrier or a supposed safe corridor.

Similar support can be provided by SEAD (suppression of enemy air defence) aircraft and by AWACS (airborne warning and control system) platforms. SEAD missions were pioneered by the Wild Weasel generations of the USAF, successively flown by the F-100F, F-105G, F-4G and specially equipped F-16C/D. By detecting and (hopefully) destroying hostile radars and other air-defence systems, these are intended to clear the way for the following attack aircraft. In the same way, the E-3 Sentry AWACS and similar aircraft, such as the E-2C Hawkeye, can assist attack forces by monitoring

Above: The Fairchild A-10A is the extreme example of the attack aircraft designed to survive AAA fire.

11

MODERN ATTACK AIRCRAFT

hostile air and defence activity and carrying out real-time calculations of optimized tracks for friendly forces, both on the way in to the target and during egress from it. What has not yet been explained is how the enemy is to be prevented from destroying all these supporting aircraft.

Of course, the crucial attack phase of the mission is strongly influenced by the weapons. Smart (precision-guided) aircraft using free-fall bombs make sense only where pinpoint accuracy is not essential and where defence firepower is known to be minimal. Where it is essential for ordnance to hit a small target, some form of sustained guidance is required all the way to impact. This can be achieved in many ways including self-homing "launch-and-forget" missiles. Such weapons obviate the need for the aircraft ever to go near the

Above: Designed as the ultimate attack aircraft, the F-111F later received Pave Tack and smart weapons.

target. One group of such missiles are those designed for use against ships, though some of this category require sustained illumination of the target by the launch aircraft's radar, which is a serious shortcoming.

Until recently, most tactical ASMs (air/surface missiles) had quite limited ranges, of the order of 5-20 miles (8-32km), in contrast to large strategic cruise missiles with ranges typically up to 1,500 miles (2,500km). Today, however, a wide range of ASMs is becoming available for tactical aircraft with stand-off ranges of 100 miles (160km) or more. Examples include ASMP and the MSOW (modular stand-off weapon).

STRUCTURE AND AERODYNAMICS

THERE IS a long and, indeed, proud heritage of attack missions being flown by aircraft designed as fighters or bombers, but which just happened to be very good aircraft. Examples include the Beaufighter, Mosquito, Ju.88, Typhoon, Canberra/B-57, F-4 Phantom II, F-16 and now the Mirage 2000N and F-15E. Thus, within limits, the structure and aerodynamics of an attack aircraft can often be those originally intended for a fighter or bomber. Today, however, the overriding need for an attack aircraft to penetrate at very low level in order to have a good chance of surviving to attack its target has had a major impact on the fundamental design of such aircraft.

To retain acceptably smooth ride qualities at high speed at low level, it is essential for attack aircraft to have the highest possible wing loading (in other words, the smallest possible wing area for any given aircraft weight) and the smallest possible wing span. This is in direct conflict with the need for air-combat fighters to have the biggest wing possible, in order to outmanoeuvre the enemy. Thus, it follows immediately that such aircraft as the Mirage 2000N, F-15E Strike Eagle and F/A-18 Hornet are inherently unsuitable for the modern attack mission.

The ideal, of course, is to use a wing that can change its shape. With the variable-geometry "swing wing", it is possible to take-off with the wings outstretched to each side and deploying high-lift leading-edge slats and double-slotted trailing-edge flaps right across the large span. Without such wings, Tornado IDS and the Su-24 could never be launched from their bases. As it is, Tornado can tote 19,840lb (9,000kg) of weapons and still need "less than 900m" (2,950ft) of runway.

Conversely, a wing like this would be a disaster for low-level penetration, but in this regime the wings are folded back to their maximum angle of 67° for Tornado and 68° for the Su-24. This tailors the aircraft perfectly to the challenging requirements of sustained maximum speed at "tree-top

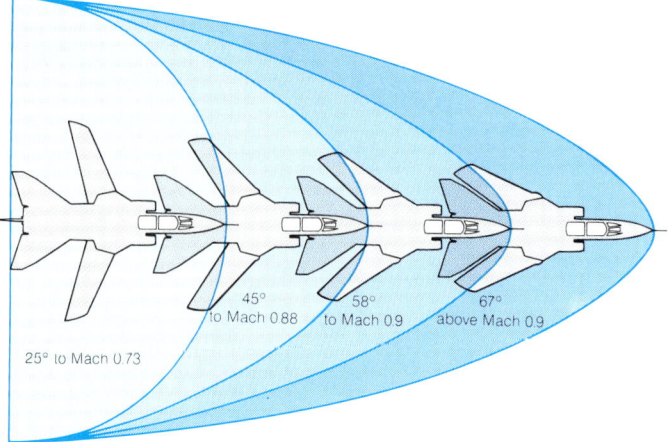

Above: Tornado, like the F-111 and Su-24, can redesign itself to match the flight Mach number (see text).

Introduction

height". Wing loading is a maximum, span is a minimum and the crew can sit back and enjoy the smooth ride. Aircraft with fixed wings give the crew such a rough time that their ability to fly the mission is seriously degraded.

It so happens that, for a decade or so, the swing wing has been out of fashion. This is largely because all the emphasis has been on warplanes designed primarily for close air combat, which, in the author's opinion, is a nonsensical policy that, with luck, will trade aircraft 1-for-1, provided the enemy forgets to wipe out our air power before it takes off. Air-combat fighters are no way to plan the basic design of an attack aircraft, which need roughly half as much wing and half as much engine thrust for any given weight. Yet even the IAI Lavi, which was intended as an attack aircraft first and an air-combat fighter second, was designed with a fixed-geometry delta wing. As for the F/A-18 Hornet, the other modern dual-role aircraft, this has a wing that is virtually the same aerodynamically as that planned for the YF-17 lightweight fighter. The author has yet to see published figures for the speed of this aircraft at sea level with maximum bombload and the number of severe vertical gusts (bumps) encountered per second. To him, it seems almost beyond belief that people can spend so much money on aircraft intended for attack missions without such fundamental matters coming to the surface.

In the author's view, there seems to be a remarkable reluctance among some nations — and the United States in particular — to accept the very unpalatable fact, that, when it comes to a shooting war, enemies are inclined to shoot back. The information that the B-1B can let go a load of 84 Mk.82 GP bombs leaves him merely puzzled. How does it propose to get anywhere near the release point?

Fortunately, all modern bombers also carry various kinds of cruise missile and these increase the probability of the aircraft returning from its mission and also have some hope of reaching their target. Modern attack aircraft can also usually carry self-guided missiles, though in some cases the aircraft has to hang about to help the missile, for example, by designating the target with a laser until the weapon hits. There are very few missiles carried by tactical aircraft that are clever enough to be released less than 100ft above the ground and then fly 100 miles or so to either a point target, such as a bridge, or a moving target such as an army or warship.

In due course, the US Navy will progressively disclose design features of the ATA (Advanced Tactical Aircraft), the contract for which was won (to Grumman's chagrin) by General Dynamics and McDonnell Douglas with the A-12A. Unquestionably, this will be the world's most advanced attack aircraft and it is frustrating to report that at present details pertaining to the A-12A are totally classified.

WEAPONS

BY THE END of World War 1, attack aircraft had flown with such diverse weapons as large batteries of rifle-calibre machine guns, fixed or manually-aimed shell-firing cannon, bombs ranging from grenades up to "thousand-pounders", rockets and even showers of steel darts that could pierce a steel helmet. Even air-launched guided missiles had been tested, from bombers and airships.

Since then we have not added much to the list, though the technology has changed dramatically. In particular, the aiming accuracy of guns and the delivery accuracy of other ordnance has been dramatically enhanced by modern avionics, though designers continue to be uncertain how far to use "smart" aircraft to deliver "dumb" weapons or to use rather ordinary aircraft to carry long-range stand-off attack missiles with pinpoint accuracy. Clearly (it seems), if you have a pinpoint weapon you do not also need a high-precision aircraft. One recalls the story of a newly arrived F-111A pilot at Takhli AB who was asked "Do you people have smart bombs?" and who replied "No, we have smart airplanes". Certainly, the fashion has been very much in favour of putting the smartness into the manned vehicle.

Above: The Harrier II can carry Sidewinders, rocket launchers and an assortment of free-fall weapons.

MODERN ATTACK AIRCRAFT

If we think back 30 years, we arrive in an era in which the attention of military staffs was focussed on missiles and, especially, on ICBMs (inter-continental ballistic missiles) and anti-ICBM defence systems. In Britain, the fixation on missiles had gone so far that in April 1957 the Minister for Defence announced that the RAF was "unlikely to require" any further fighters or bombers and that "work on such aircraft will stop". In other words, the smartness was in 1957 being transferred to the missiles 100 per cent.

While retaining large stocks of 20mm guns and ammunition, the RAF's attack aircraft comprise the Jaguar and Harrier I with two guns of 30mm calibre, the Tornado with two guns of 27mm and the Harrier II with two guns of 25mm. Obviously, it would be more sensible to use a single type of gun in all these aircraft, if possible of a type employing ammunition that was standard throughout NATO.

There seems to be no argument over the need for guns in attack aircraft. Indeed, in the case of specialised tank-killers, the whole aircraft can be designed around a single gun of tremendous power. Another factor worth noting is that, while the make-up of the ammunition may be the same for both the air/air and air/ground missions, the rate of fire may not. For example, the MW27 gun fitted to Tornado can be set to 1,000 shots/min for ground attack or to 1,700 for air/air, while the DEFA 554 30mm gun can be set to 1,100 for air/ground or 1,800 for air/air.

Today, free-fall or unguided stores can be obtained in a bewildering variety. Plain bombs exist in traditional bluff shapes and also as "slicks", which differ only in being more streamlined. Thus, when carried in quantity, they impose a reduced performance penalty on the aircraft while to some degree their ballistic properties also give improved aiming accuracy. The need to drop bombs from very low altitude led to the need for some form of retarding mechanism as long ago as World War 2, to give the attacking aircraft a chance of avoiding damage from its own bombs. Clearly, retarded bombs have to be used with care when it is planned to attack a point target with aircraft spaced out in line ahead! Some bombs have in-built airbrakes while others use small parachutes. The timing and characteristics of the drag device must be precisely repeatable if there is not to be an unacceptably large along-track aiming error.

The only other weapons designed to be released on surface targets from very low level — apart from chemical, biological and incendiary stores — are those which dispense bomblets, grenades and similar "scatter" devices, which may be designed to pierce armour, attack hard targets generally, kill infantry in the open or perform various other functions. Again, there is great diversity. The Swiss CH-TABO pod releases a stream of small spherical self-braked bombs, each of which can be triggered by a radar altimeter or by ground contact to disperse 8,000 steel balls each able to penetrate 5mm of steel. The French Belouga pod dispenses 151 grenades under cartridge power in 16 radial directions, each grenade being chosen from three types: general attack (fragmentation), armour piercing or area interdiction (against harbours, marshalling yards and similar large targets). The French BM 400 is released as one unit and then at preset times ejects three anti-armour modules each of which explodes into fragments, either 800 fragments penetrating 17mm of armour at 50m (164ft) range or 1,500 fragments penetrating 12mm at the same distance. The bulky German MW-1 system carried by Tornado comprises four boxes with a total of 112 transverse tubes, whose 224 muzzles (112 to left of track, 112 on the right) can shoot out 4,536 anti-armour bomblets on one pass, or a wide variety of other stores such as anti-airfield munitions.

Another German weapon, the VBW, comprises a pod complete with its own anti-armour sensing system, which from a height of 250ft (76m) scans a band of terrain about 100ft (30m) wide. No matter how fast the aircraft is flying, the VBW automatically fires anti-armour projectiles with great accuracy from tubes pointing downwards and to the rear on to any armoured vehicle the system detects. Another German weapon is MBB's MDS (Modular Dispenser System) which fits on any standard bomb rack and can accommodate various laterally dispensed submunitions which are fired either while the container remains attached to the aircraft, down to an attack height of 164ft (50m), or at a predetermined time after the whole container has been released. A modified MDS is being developed for the Swedish Gripen and may be carried by the AJ37 Viggen. South Africa developed the CB 470 pod which can be triggered at speeds up to 690mph (1,100km/h) at heights as low as 82ft (25m). Each releases 40 spherical

Below: Big runway-cratering and small area-denial sub-munitions pour from Tornado's JP-233 dispensers.

14

bombs which hit the ground, bounce (even from mud or water) and explode 0.65second later to scatter fragments at about 4,260ft (1,300m)/sec. A single CB 470 covers a footprint 230ft (70m) wide by 820ft (250m) long. In Britain, Hunting's BL.755 has been widely adopted in two main versions, each scattering 147 anti-armour (shaped-charge) bomblets. The same company produces the large JP.233 anti-airfield dispenser loaded with a mix of runway-cratering submunitions and area-denial submunitions, while the Hades is essentially nothing more than the BL.755 loaded with the JP.233 type anti-personnel area-denial munitions.

Guided ASMs (air/surface missiles) date from 1917, but were first used in large numbers by the Luftwaffe in World War II. In the late 1950s, the US Navy began the modern era with Bullpup, which was originally a 250lb bomb with crude guidance by radio command signals from the launch aircraft, by an operator who tried to keep bright flares on the missile lined up with the target. As it forced the attacking aircraft to cruise in close proximity to the target until the missile hit, this was in some ways worse than "iron bombs", but today there are numerous smart (self-contained precision guidance) missiles and bombs, as well as some brilliant ones (which can detect targets and home on to whichever presents the greatest threat, whilst ignoring any target that has been picked out by another weapon already). To the enemy, at least, there is no real difference between an ASM and a smart bomb, though the latter are essentially ordinary bombs to which have been added a target-homing sensor in the nose and control fins to steer the bomb on to the target.

STEALTH AND THE FUTURE

THERE IS just one way in which the need to fly smoothly at near the speed of sound at sea level can be sidestepped and that is by making the aircraft "stealthy". If the aircraft can be made virtually undetectable, by sight, by radar, by IR emission and by sound, then all previous considerations fly out of the window and we can safely let the shape be dictated by the stealth requirements. Thus, the F-117A has a shape and propulsion system designed to make it undetectable, without worrying about how fast it flies. In the same way, while the B-1B (a design making important concessions to LO but whose basic shape was decided long beforehand) has afterburners and VG swing wings, the Northrop B-2 has a very special long-span fixed wing and no afterburners. The author will be intrigued to see how the new Advanced Tactical Fighters, the Lockheed/GD/Boeing YF-22A and Northrop/McDonnell Douglas YF-23A, have been designed. These aircraft are primarily not intended for attack missions. On the other hand, the Advanced Tactical Aircraft, the GD/McDonnell Douglas A-12A, will unquestionably be a 100 per cent stealth aircraft. In consequence, it will make no pretensions at supersonic speed and is almost certain to have two unaugmented (and very quiet) turbofan engines as well as an internal bomb bay.

Stealth design does not remove the need to fly fast but it eases the pressure greatly. This not only changes the necessary shape of the aircraft but also greatly reduces the severity of the ride, as previously explained, which in turn reduces the rapidity with which the structure accumulates fatigue damage. In the traditional US style of surface attack, in which the aircraft cruises to the target well above ground level at less than full throttle and then dives on the target, the incidence of fatigue is very low and not even as severe as in the air-combat mission. In the full-throttle ground level mission, it is a totally different story. The first (and almost only) US aircraft to fly such missions was the F-111. This suffered 11 years of fatigue problems, which were several times responsible for catastrophic accidents and even today the Sacramento Air Logistics Center and British Aerospace include structural rework in their F-111 refurbishment contracts. In Britain, the very first aircraft to be designed for sustained sea level flight at maximum speed, the Buccaneer, has suffered a severe setback from fatigue in recent years, while its direct counterpart in the USA, the A-6E Intruder, is having to be completely rewinged, even though Grumman has a proud reputation for structural strength.

The author expects the wing of the A-12A to be entirely made of composite materials, predominantly graphite-fibre based. Such materials are now sufficiently well understood to be trusted with primary structure, as for example in the entire wing of the Harrier II, and they are good for stealth and have virtually no known fatigue problem. Parts that are not made of composites in modern warplanes are likely to be mainly of aluminium/lithium alloy.

Apart from the fact that it has a blended wing/fuselage, high butterfly (V-type) tail and unfamiliar non-reflective angles all over, the Lockheed F-117A remains an enigma. It seems obvious that the engines must be lost inside the giant over-wing cowlings, whose purpose is certainly to surround them with a large secondary airflow to reduce IR signature and noise. Obviously, the arrangement of the engines and cowling, perhaps plus added internal baffles, prevents the engine faces from being seen by radars ahead of the aircraft. What remains under wraps is what kind of radar-absorbing surface coating is used and whether this has any chameleon-like ability to change colour at visual wavelengths. The aircraft in the only released photograph looked very dark and stood out clearly from the light background.

MODERN ATTACK AIRCRAFT

Aeritalia/Aermacchi/ EMBRAER AMX

This machine's designation stems from Aeritalia/Macchi Xperimental, and it was started in 1977 as an Italian study project for a replacement for the G91 and F-104G. The eminently sensible decision was taken to aim at a subsonic limiting Mach number, the result being an aircraft that promises to be light, compact, relatively cheap, possessed of good short-field performance, versatile in operation and capable of carrying a wide assortment of equipment and weapons. In some respects it resembles a modernized Hunter, though of course it represents a different level of technology in aerodynamics, structure and systems. The participation of the Brazilian partner has not only broadened the market and manufacturing base but also expanded the variety of equipment and weapons fits.

The basic AM-X will be used chiefly in tactical roles such as close air support and battlefield interdiction, operating with full fuel and weapons from unpaved strips. The design has attempted to maximize reliability and the ability to withstand battle damage, and to an exceptional extent everything on board is modular and quickly replaceable. The seat is a Martin-Baker 10L, fuel is divided between the fuselage and wings, and flight controls are dual hydraulic with manual back-up.

The two original customers have specified simple range-only radars of different types. The Italian aircraft, of which 187 are planned to be delivered to the AMI to equip eight squadrons, will have a high standard of avionics, with a HUD, INS and Tacan, digital data highways and processing, an advanced cockpit display and a very comprehensive ECM installation. Any of three different photo-recon modules can

Above: An AMX featuring the markings of the Aeronautica Militare's 8th Stormo, based at Cervia San Giorgio.

Aeritalia/Aermacchi/EMBRAER AMX

Origin: Joint programme by Aeritalia/Aermacchi of Italy, and EMBRAER of Brazil.
Engine: One 11,030lb (5,003kg) Rolls-Royce Spey 807 turbofan produced in Italy under licence by Fiat, Piaggio and Alfa Romeo.
Dimensions: Span (over AAMs), 32ft 9.75in (10.0m); length 44ft 6.5in (13.575m); height 15ft 0.25in (4.576m); wing area 226sq ft (21.0m²).
Weights: Empty 14,770lb (6,700kg); max loaded 27,558lb (12,500kg).
Performance: Max speed with external load at sea level 654mph (1,052km/h, Mach 0.86); cruising speed Mach 0.75 to 0.8; takeoff run at max weight 3,120ft (950m); attack radius with reserves with 6,000lb (2,722kg) of ordnance (hi-lo-hi) 320 miles (570km), (lo-lo-lo) 230 miles (370km).
Armament: Total of 8,377lb (3,800kg) carried on centreline pylon, four underwing pylons and AAM wingtip rails; internal gun(s) (Italy) one 20mm M61A-1 with 350 rounds, (Brazil) two 30mm DEFA 5.54 with 125 rounds each.
History: Start of design studies 1977; first flight (Italy) 1984, (Brazil) 1985.

be installed in a large bay in the lower right side of the fuselage, while an external IR/optronics recon pod can be carried on the centreline pylon.

The Brazilian FAB expects to acquire 79, with VOR/ILS but no INS, different guns and other avionic variations. The original FAB force requirement was for 144, and it is possible that this may be restored.

Flight development was satisfactory, and the first series production AMX flew on 11 May 1988. Deliveries are expected to continue until 1994, extended by any possible export orders. Meanwhile, in 1986 work began on a tandem two-seat version, with the rear cockpit replacing the forward fuel tank. This version is envisaged as a trainer, electronic-warfare platform or maritime attack aircraft.

Left: Seven prototypes were built, three being assembled by Aeritalia and two each by Aermacchi and EMBRAER. Each carried a nose insignia for the three partners.

Right: Underside of the 8th Stormo AMX, with two 2,000lb and two 1,000lb bombs, two Durandal and two AIM-9L Sidewinder air-to-air self-defence missiles.

MODERN ATTACK AIRCRAFT

Aermacchi M.B.339

Origin: Aermacchi SpA, Italy.
Engine: One Rolls-Royce Viper turbojet built under licence in Italy, with manufacture of parts by Fiat and assembly and test by Piaggio; (326K and 339A) 4,000lb (1,814kg) Viper 632-43; (339K) 4,450lb (2,019kg) Viper 680.
Dimensions: Span (over tip tanks) 35ft 7.48in (10.858m), length 35ft 11.96in (10.972m), height 13ft 1.24in (3,994m); wing area 207.7sq ft (10.3m²).
Weights: Empty (A) 6,889lb (3,125kg); max (326K and 339A) 12,996lb (5,895kg), (K) 13,558lb (6,150kg).
Performance: Max speed (clean, S/L) (326K and 339A) 558mph (898km/h), (K) 564mph (907km/h), takeoff run at max wt (A) 3,000ft (915m), (K) 2,986ft (910m); combat radius (both, with four Mk 82 bombs, lo-lo-lo) 230 miles (371km).
Armament: (326A and 339A): Up to 4,000lb (1,814kg) carried on six underwing pylons; the centre station on each wing being plumbed for a 71.5gal (325lit) tank, stores including AIM-9 or Magic AAMs and two pods each containing either a 30mm DEFA 5-53 gun and 120 rounds or a 12.7mm M3 with 350 rounds, (K) internal installation of two 30mm DEFA 5-53 guns each with 120 rounds, and maximum of 4,270lb (1,937kg) of external weapons carried on same six underwing hardpoints.
History: Original M.B.326 first flew on 10 December 1957; 339 prototype first flew 12 August 1976; first delivery of 339A for service trials 8 August 1979. Company 339K first flew 30 May 1980.

The M.B.339 is a modernized development of the best-selling M.B.326 tandem jet trainer, hundreds of which are in use all over the world. The 326K introduced a strengthened and uprated model, with fuel replacing the rear cockpit and powerful inbuilt armament. The Atlas Impala 2 combines this airframe with the original lower-powered Rolls-Royce Viper 540 turbojet engine.

Compared with the 326 the 339 has a revised airframe, the most significant change being the provision of a raised rear cockpit for the instructor. The cockpit is pressurized and

Below: Side elevation of an M.B.339A of the Dubai Air Wing of the UAE (United Arab Emirates) air force, which bought two in 1984.

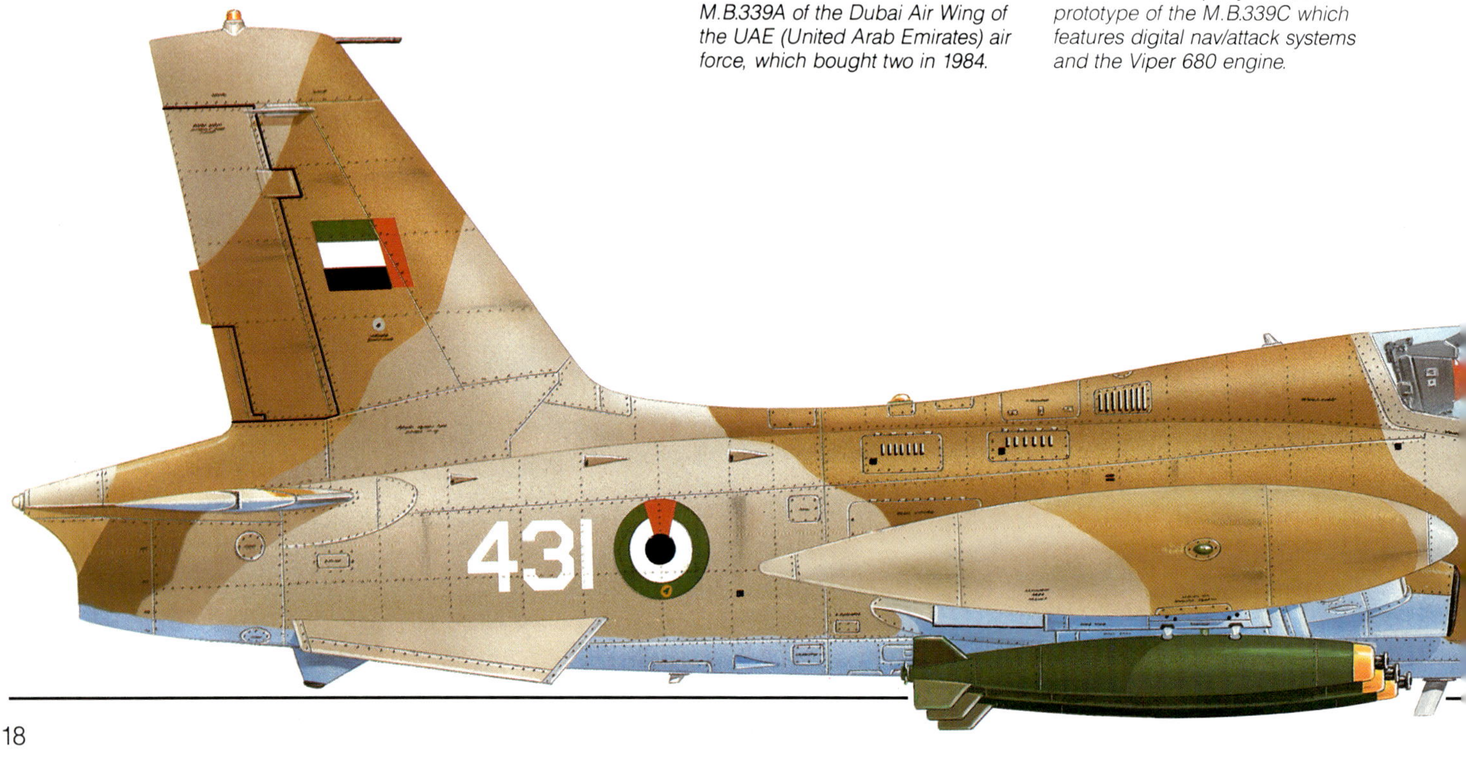

Above: The company-owned prototype of the M.B.339C which features digital nav/attack systems and the Viper 680 engine.

Aermacchi M.B.339

fitted with Martin-Baker Mk 10 zero/zero seats, and standard avionics include Tacan, VOR, DME and ILS and a Marconi dead-reckoning computer.

In 1982 the Italian Air Force received some camouflaged M.B.339As, and these are intended for use as part of an emergency close air support force. The lower powered 339A, however, cannot really succeed in such missions except in third-world visual environments (where its low price is attractive). The IndAer company of Peru hopes to build a large number under licence and may be permitted to export in certain markets. The Italian Air Force aerobatic team, Frecce Tricolori, uses a version designated M.B.339PAN.

Aermacchi has upgraded the performance with a more powerful single-seat model, the 339K Veltro 2 (Veltro, Greyhound, was the name of a famed Macchi fighter of World War II). This is offered with such customer options as a HUD, TV type display and integral ECM installation. In 1988 Aermacchi was studying the possibility of developing a specialized twin-engined (JT15D engines) version of the M.B.339 for the USAF.

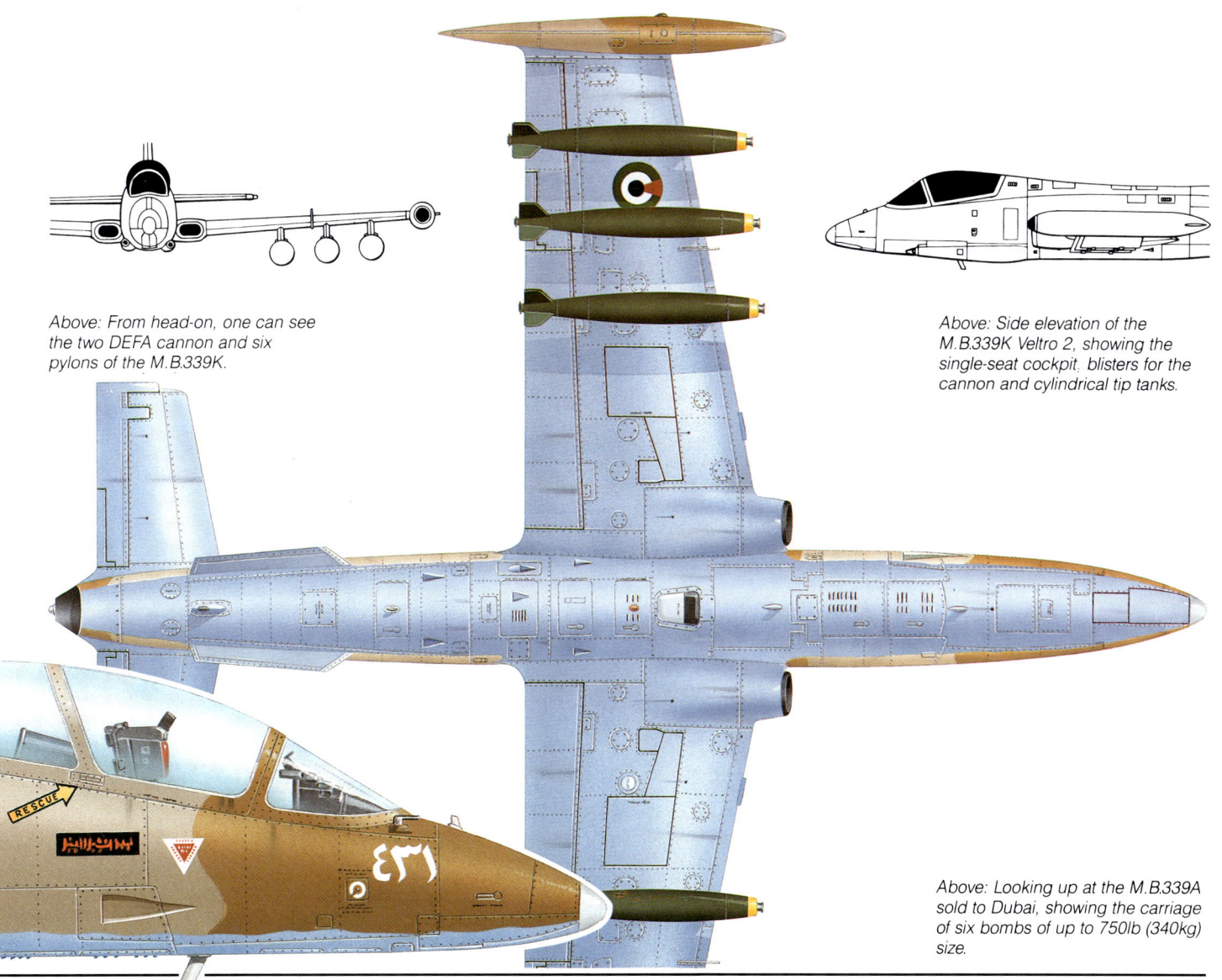

Above: From head-on, one can see the two DEFA cannon and six pylons of the M.B.339K.

Above: Side elevation of the M.B.339K Veltro 2, showing the single-seat cockpit, blisters for the cannon and cylindrical tip tanks.

Above: Looking up at the M.B.339A sold to Dubai, showing the carriage of six bombs of up to 750lb (340kg) size.

19

MODERN ATTACK AIRCRAFT

British Aerospace Buccaneer

Origin: British Aerospace (originally Blackburn, later Hawker Siddeley), UK.
Engines: Two 11,030lb (5,003kg) Rolls-Royce Spey 101 turbofans.
Dimensions: Span 44ft (13.41m); length 63ft 5in (19.33m); height 16ft 3in (4.95m); wing area 514.7sq ft (47.82m²).
Weights: Empty about 30,000lb (13,610kg); maximum loaded 62,000lb (28,123kg).
Performance: Max speed 690mph (1,110km/h) at sea level; range on typical hi-lo-hi strike mission with weapon load 2,300 miles (3,700km).
Armament: Rotating bomb door carries four 1,000lb (454kg) bombs or multisensor reconnaissance pack or 440gal tank; four wing pylons each stressed to 3,000lb (1,361kg), compatible with guided and/or free-fall missiles. Total load 16,000lb (7,257kg).
History: First flight (NA.39) 30 April 1958, (production S.1) 23 January 1962, (prototype S.2) 17 May 1963, (production S.2) 5 June 1964, final delivery late 1975.

In April 1957 the notorious "Defence White Paper" proclaimed manned combat aircraft obsolete. Subsequently the Blackburn B.103, built to meet the naval attack specification NA.39, was the only new British military aircraft that was not cancelled. Designed for carrier operation, its wing and tail were dramatically reduced in size as a result of powerful tip-to-tip supercirculation (BLC, boundary-layer control) achieved by blasting hot compressed air bled from the engines from narrow slits. The S.1 (strike Mk 1) was marginal on power, but the greatly improved S.2 was a reliable and formidable aircraft.

The first 84 were ordered by the Royal Navy but, when the government ordered the phase-out of Britain's conventional carrier force, most were transferred to RAF Strike Command, designated S.2B when converted to launch Martel missiles. The RAF signed in 1968 for 43 new S.2Bs with new avionics and probe.

Within the limits of crippling budgets the RAF Buccaneers have been updated by a few improved avionics, and have gradually been recognized as among the world's best long-range interdiction aircraft. When carrying a 4,000-lb (1,814kg)

Below: Side elevation of XV359, a Buccaneer S.2C which in 1984 was serving with No.12 Squadron while deployed to RAF Akrotiri, Cyprus for weapons training. The Mk.2C designation refers to ex-RN aircraft not equipped to launch Martel missiles.

British Aerospace Buccaneer

bombload a "Bucc" at full power is faster than a Mirage, Phantom or F-16 at low level, and burns less fuel per mile. Many Red Flag exercises have demonstrated that a well-flown example is among the most difficult of all today's aircraft to shoot down. On most occasions an intercepting aircraft has failed to get within missile or gun-firing parameters before having to abandon the chase because of low fuel state. Almost universally the Buccaneer aircrews consider that "the only replacement for a Buccaneer in the 1990s will be another Buccaneer, with updated avionics".

In fact this is just what the RAF is getting. Though most Buccaneer squadrons have re-equipped with Tornados, 42 S.2Bs are being updated by British Aerospace to fit them for many years of further service in the maritime role, using Sea Eagle and Martel missiles. The update involves a careful structural audit to avoid future fatigue, and installation of FIN 1063 inertial navigation, an upgraded Blue Parrot radar, MDS Guardrail radar warning and ESM, Tracor ALE-40 chaff/flare dispensers and new Plessey radios. The aircraft were due to be redelivered to maritime strike units of the Royal Air Force during the course of 1987-89.

Above: One of the S.2Bs that was built for the RAF, with 425-gal weapon-door tank, FR probe and a number of other detail improvements.

Right: Underside view of the same aircraft, showing two 430-gal slipper tanks, one AIM-9G self-defence missile and an ALQ-101 electronic countermeasures pod.

MODERN ATTACK AIRCRAFT

British Aerospace Harrier and Sea Harrier

Origin: British Aerospace, UK.
Engine: One 21,500lb (9,752kg) thrust Rolls-Royce Pegasus vectored-thrust turbofan.
Dimensions: Span 25ft 3in (7.7m); length (H) 47ft 2in (14.38m), (SH) 47ft 7in (14.5m); height 12ft 2in (3.71m); wing area 201.1sq ft (18.68m²).
Weights: Empty, (H) 12,200lb (5,533kg), (SH) 12,250lb (5,557kg); max (non-VTOL) (H) 25,200lb (11,430kg), (SH) 26,200lb (11,880kg).
Performance: Max speed 737mph (1,186km/h); typical lo attack speed 690mph (1,110km/h); hi intercept radius (3min combat plus reserves and vertical landing) 460 miles (750km); lo strike radius 288 miles (463km).
Armament: Two 30mm Aden Mk 4 each with 150 rounds; five hardpoints for max load of 8,000lb (3,630kg) including Sea Eagle or Harpoon ASMs, Sidewinder AAMs and wide range of other stores.
History: First flight (H) 28 December 1967, (SH) 20 August 1978; first squadron (H) April 1969, (SH) 19 September 1979.

Until May 1982 the Harrier was generally regarded (except by those familar with it) as a quaint toy of an experimental nature. Since then it has become a battle-proven weapon which sustained intensive operations in conditions which would have kept other aircraft grounded.

When the experimental P.1127 got daylight under its wheels in 1960 the RAF showed not the slightest interest (in any case, British combat aircraft had been officially pronounced obsolete). Gradually this became the Harrier, a machine of classic simplicity which pioneered the entire concept of STOVL (short takeoff, vertical landing) combat operations, and the sustained mounting of close-support and recon missions from dispersed sites.

Though not designed as a fighter, its combination of small size, unusual shape, lack of visible smoke and unique agility make even the original Harrier a most unpopular opponent for any modern interceptor.

The RAF Harrier GR.3 has an inertial nav/attack system laser ranger and marked-target seeker and fin-mounted passive warning receivers. It is planned to install internal ECM.

After years of delay the Sea Harrier developed from the Harrier chiefly by redesigning the forward fuselage. The deeper structure provides for a Ferranti Blue Fox radar, which folds 180deg for shipboard stowage, and a new cockpit with space for a much-enhanced nav/attack/combat system.

The Royal Navy purchased 57 FRS.1s, the designation meaning "fighter, recon, strike". In the NATO context the main task is air defence at all heights, normally with direction from surface vessels, either as DLI (deck-launched intercept) or CAP (combat air patrol). In the Falklands 28 Sea Harriers repeatedly demonstrated their ability to fly six sorties a day in extremely severe weather, destroying 22 Argentine aircraft. Many new techniques were demonstrated including

Below: Harrier GR.3 XZ997 fought in the Falklands with No.1 Squadron. It still serves with the RAF but will be replaced by a GR.5/7.

Right: From the underside, XZ997 can be seen to be carrying two 30mm Aden gun pods plus a pair of Mk.13/13 LGBs (laser-guided bombs).

British Aerospace Harrier and Sea Harrier

4,000-mile (6,440km) flights and operations from quickly added sheet laid on containers in a merchant ship.

Under a mid-life improvement programme, the Royal Navy FRS.1 aircraft are being updated to have lookdown-shootdown capability with a new radar of pulse-doppler type, named Blue Vixen. This will considerably upgrade all-round capability, and in particular will match the range of the new Sea Eagle anti-ship missile. It is expected that Zeus active ECM will be installed, together with pairs of AIM-120A (Amraam) AAMs, and the cockpit will be updated.

The only export customer so far is the Indian Navy. This service purchased 23 FRS.51 and four T.60 two-seat trainers. They operate with No. 300 Sqn from shore bases and from INS *Vikrant* and *Viraat*.

Left: In side view, the RAF Harrier GR.3 differs from today's GR.5 in having the small nose and low canopy, plus tip-mounted outriggers.

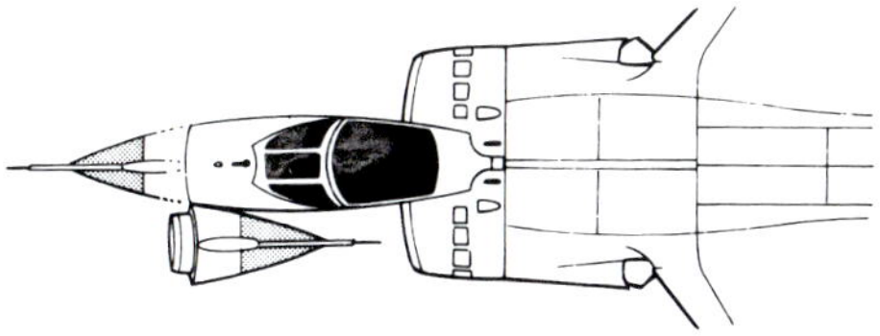

Below: Unlike RAF aircraft, the Royal Navy Sea Harrier has radar in the nose which can fold through 180 deg to fit British carriers.

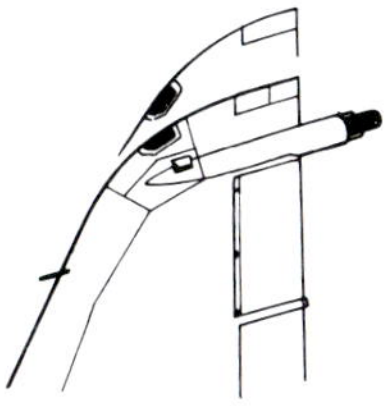

Below: Early Harriers have the outrigger almost at the wingtips but for long range a bolt-on tip can be added.

MODERN ATTACK AIRCRAFT

British Aerospace Hawk

Origin: British Aerospace, UK.
Engine: One 5,845lb (2,651kg) Rolls-Royce Turbomeca Adour Mk 871 turbofan.
Dimensions: Span 30ft 10in (9.4m); length (100, over probe) 39ft 2.5in (11.95m) (200) 37ft 4in (11.38m); height 13ft 5in (4.09m); wing area 179.54sq ft (16.69m²).
Weights: Empty (100) 8,500lb (3,855kg), (200) 9,100lb (4,128kg); max loaded (100) 18,890lb (8,570kg), (200) 20,065lb (9,101kg).
Performance: Max speed 644mph (1,037km/h) at low level; Mach number in shallow dive 1.2; initial climb 11,800ft (3,600m)/min; service ceiling 50,000ft (15,240m); combat radius (100 with 5,000lb, 2,268kg weapons) 620 miles (1,000km); ferry range 2,530 miles (4,075km).
Armament: (100) Up to 7,200lb (3,265kg) including 30mm gun pod; (200) one or two internal 25mm guns and 7,700lb (3,500kg) offensive stores.
History: First flight 21 August 1974; service delivery 1976.

Above: 72 of the RAF's Hawks are declared to NATO in the local-defence fighter role. Designated T.1A, they may be armed with the inra-red homing AIM-9 Sidewinder air-to-air missile.

Below: Side elevation of one of the 60 Hawk 200 single-seaters being supplied to the Royal Saudi Air Force. These are among the most versatile combat aircraft in the world.

The RAF ordered 175 Hawk T.1 trainers, all delivered by 1982. In 1981 it was announced that, to back up RAF Strike Command's fighter defence forces, 88 would be equipped to fire AIM-9L Sidewinders in the light interception role. Under current planning about 72 T.1As are actually armed.

In addition the Hawk was selected in 1981 as the future undergraduate pilot trainer of the US Navy, as the T-45A Goshawk; 302 are required.

Most of the export customers other than the US Navy use their Hawks in at least a weapons training role, and some task them with combat missions. BAe is marketing a Series 100 dedicated attack version of the Hawk with digital avionics, inertial navigation, wide-angle HUDs in both cockpits, Hotas controls, colour multifunction displays, an advanced weapon management system, passive radar warning, optional FLIR and laser ranger in a chisel nose and provision for an ECM pod. The first Hawk 100 flew in October 1987.

In June 1984 British Aerospace announced the Hawk 200, a single-seat multirole combat variant, and the first production Hawk 200 flew on 24 April 1987. Except for having a taller fin, the 200 is similar to earlier models aft of the cockpit. Tremendous variations are possible for almost every kind of tactical mission, the nose being able to accommodate either FLIR/laser or a multimode radar such as the Westinghouse APG-66. In nearly all versions two 25mm Aden guns, each with 100 rounds, are mounted under the cockpit floor, freeing the centreline pylon for a 130gal (592 litre) drop tank. Each of the four wing pylons is stressed for a 2,000lb (907kg) load. Saudi Arabia has ordered 60 Hawk 200s.

British Aerospace Hawk

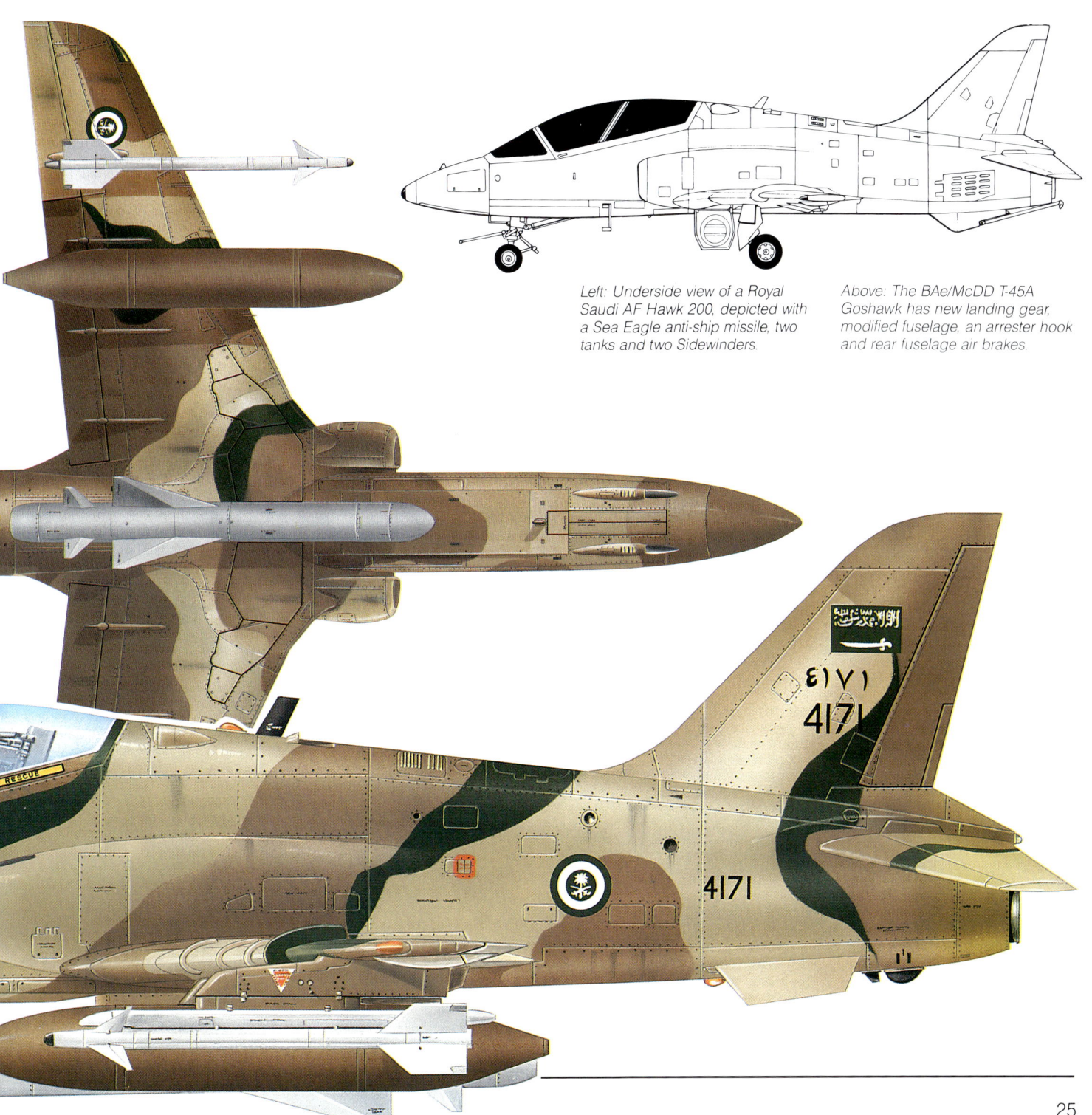

Left: Underside view of a Royal Saudi AF Hawk 200, depicted with a Sea Eagle anti-ship missile, two tanks and two Sidewinders.

Above: The BAe/McDD T-45A Goshawk has new landing gear, modified fuselage, an arrester hook and rear fuselage air brakes.

MODERN ATTACK AIRCRAFT

British Aerospace Strikemaster

Origin: British Aerospace (originally Hunting, later BAC), UK.
Engine: 3,410lb (1,547kg) thrust Rolls-Royce Viper 535 turbojet.
Dimensions: Span 36ft 10in (11.23m); length 33ft 8.5in (10.27m); height 10ft 11.5in (3.34m).
Weights: Empty 6,270lb (2,840kg); loaded (clean) 9,200lb (4,170kg); max 11,500lb (5,210kg).
Performance: Max speed 481mph (774km/h); max speed at sea level 450mph (726km/h); initial climb (max fuel, clean) 5,250ft(1,600m)/min; service ceiling 44,000ft (13,410m); ferry range 1,615 miles (2,600km); combat radius with 3,300lb weapon load 145 miles (233km).
Armament: Two 7.62mm FN machine guns fixed firing forwards with 550 rounds each; wide range of stores to max of 3,000lb (1,360kg) on four underwing strong points.
History: First flight (Jet Provost) 16 June 1954; (Strikemaster) 26 October 1967; first delivery 1968.

The roots of this cost effective machine go back to the Percival Provost basic trainer, flown in February 1950. Hunting then produced a jet version, and flew this in June 1954. Subsequently the Hunting (later BAC) Jet Provost became a successful basic trainer made in great numbers for the RAF and many overseas countries.

From the pressurized Jet Provost T.5 was developed the BAC.145 multirole trainer/attack aircraft, which in turn was developed into the highly refined Strikemaster. With a more powerful Viper engine, the Strikemaster proved to be a great worldwide success. It has side-by-side ejection seats, and the ability to operate from the roughest airstrip whilst carrying a combat load three times a typical bomber's load in the 1930s and any desired equipment fit. The Strikemaster has set a world record for the number of repeat orders placed by its export customers.

One of the many JP export customers was the Sudan, and the air force of this country purchased three of the last ten Strikemasters. These were actually assembled at Hurn, and were delivered as new Mk 90s in 1984. One went to Oman in 1986 and the final six were supplied to Ecuador in 1988, bringing the total up to 151. Nine Strikemasters were re-purchased from Kuwait in 1986 and sold to Botswana in 1988.

Despite its modest flight performance the Strikemaster's toughness, agility, useful armament loads and low costs will keep it in customer inventories until the year 2000.

Left: The Strikemaster has equipped New Zealand's No.14 Squadron at the Ohakea base for some 20 years.

Below: Side elevation of one of the Strikemaster Mk.82s of No.1 Squadron of the Sultan of Oman's Air Force.

British Aerospace Strikemaster

Far right: Seen during a pre-delivery test flight, this Strikemaster Mk.83 was the first example to enter service with Kuwait.

Right: Underside view of the Strikemaster Mk.88 of the SOAF. It is carrying two bombs and 16 Swiss Oerlikon SURA 81mm rockets.

27

MODERN ATTACK AIRCRAFT

Cessna T-37 and A-37B Dragonfly

Origin: Cessna Aircraft Co, USA.
Engines: (T) two 1,025lb (465kg) thrust Teledyne CAE J69-25 turbojets, (A) two 2,850lb (1,293kg) thrust General Electric J85-17A turbojets.
Dimensions: Span (T) 33ft 9.3in (10.3m), (A, over tanks) 35ft 10.5in (10.93m); length (T) 29ft 3in (8.92m), (A, excl refuelling probe) 28ft 3.25in (8.62m); wing area 183.9sq ft (17.09m²).
Weights: Empty (T) 3,870lb (1,755kg), (A) 6,211lb (2,817kg); loaded (T) 6,600lb (2,993kg) (A) 14,000lb (6,350kg).
Performance: Max speed (T) 426mph (685km/h), (A) 507mph (816km/h); normal cruising speed (T) 380mph (612km/h), (A, clean) 489mph (787km/h); initial climb (T) 3,020ft (920m)/min, (A) 6,990ft (2,130m)/min; service ceiling (T) 35,100ft (10,700m), (A) 41,765ft (12,730m), range (T, 5 per cent reserves, 25,000ft/7,620m cruise) 604 miles (972km), (A, max fuel, four drop tanks) 1,012 miles (1,628km), (A, max payload including 4,100lb/1,860kg ordnance) 460 miles (740km).
Armament: (T) None, (A) GAU-2B/A 7.62mm Minigun in fuselage, eight underwing pylons (four inners 870lb/394kg each, next 600lb/272kg and outers 500lb/227kg) for large number of weapons, pods, dispensers, clusters, launchers or recon/EW equipment.
History: First flight (T) 12 October 1954, (A) 22 October 1963.

For almost 30 years the basic pilot trainer of the USAF, the T-37 uses two simple French-designed turbojets (Turbomeca Marborés) made in the USA, has stressed-skin construction and seats an instructor and pupil in side-by-side ejection seats. Export models are T-37Cs, and many have been passed on secondhand to other air forces in recent years. About 850 are in use of over 1,300 built.

The much more powerful A-37 has a strengthened airframe to carry heavy underwing and wingtip loads and still fly uninhibited manoeuvres. Surprisingly, ejection seats are not fitted to this version, which was originally created for "brushfire" wars where ground defences are primitive. Many Dragonflies have inflight-refuelling probes; about 600 were built. USAF-operated A-37B Dragonfly ground-support aircraft have been adapted (with the designation OA-37) for forward air control duty with some Air National Guard Groups. Others are serving in South Korea.

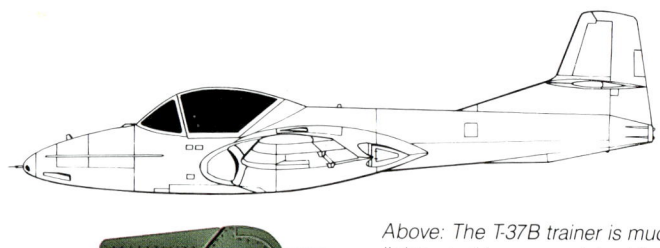

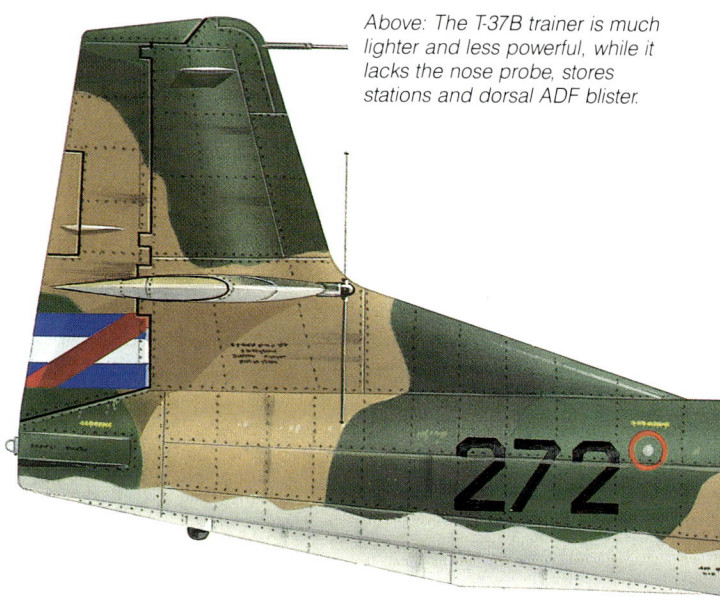

Above: The T-37B trainer is much lighter and less powerful, while it lacks the nose probe, stores stations and dorsal ADF blister.

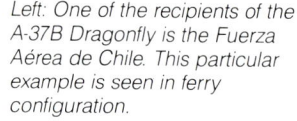

Left: One of the recipients of the A-37B Dragonfly is the Fuerza Aérea de Chile. This particular example is seen in ferry configuration.

Cessna T-37 and A-37B Dragonfly

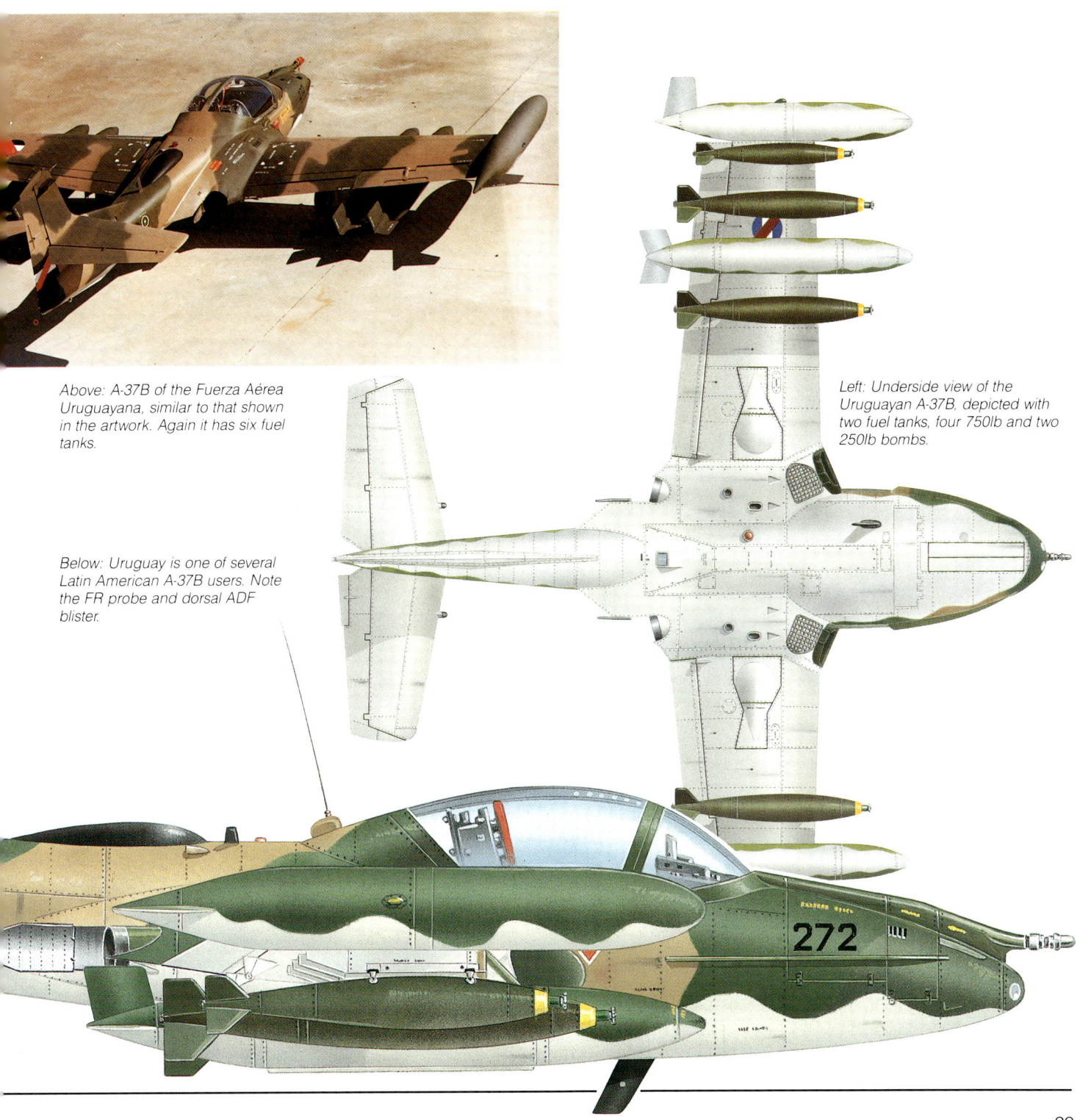

Above: A-37B of the Fuerza Aérea Uruguayana, similar to that shown in the artwork. Again it has six fuel tanks.

Below: Uruguay is one of several Latin American A-37B users. Note the FR probe and dorsal ADF blister.

Left: Underside view of the Uruguayan A-37B, depicted with two fuel tanks, four 750lb and two 250lb bombs.

29

MODERN ATTACK AIRCRAFT

Dassault-Breguet Mirage III and 5

Origin: Avions Marcel Dassault-Breguet Aviation, France.
Engine: (IIIC) 13,225lb (6,000kg) thrust (max afterburner) SNECMA Atar 9B turbojet, (most other III and some 5) 13,670lb (6,200kg) Atar 9C; (IIIR2Z, NG and 50) 15,873lb (7,200kg) Atar 9K50.
Dimensions: Span 27ft (8.22m); length (excl probe) (IIIC) 48ft 5in (14.75m), (IIIE) 49ft 3.5in (15.03m), (5) 51ft 0.25in (15.55m); height 13ft 11.5in (4.25m); wing area 375sq ft (35.0m²).
Weights: Empty (IIIC) 13,570lb (6,156kg); (IIIE) 15,540lb (7,050kg); (IIIR) 14,550lb (6,600kg); (IIIB) 13,820lb (6,270kg); (5) 14,550lb (6,600kg); loaded (IIIC) 19,700lb (8,936kg); (IIIE, IIIR, 5) 29,760lb (13,500kg), (IIIB) 26,455lb (12,000kg).
Performance: Max speed (all models, clean) 863mph (1,390km/h, Mach 1.14) at sea level, 1,460mph (2,350km/h, Mach 2.2) at altitude; initial climb, over 16,400ft (5,000m)/min (time to 36,090ft/11,000m, 3min); service ceiling (Mach 1.8) 55,775ft (17,000m), range (clean) at altitude about 1,000 miles (1,610km); combat radius in attack mission with two bombs and tanks (hi-altitude) 745 miles (1,200km); ferry range with three external tanks, 2,485 miles (4,000km).
Armament: Two 30mm DEFA 5-52 cannon, each with 125 rounds (normally fitted to all versions except when IIIC carries rocket-boost pack); three 1,000lb (454kg) external pylons for bombs, missiles or tanks (Mirage 5, seven external pylons with max capacity of 9,260lb/4,200kg).
History: First flight (prototype Mirage III-001) 17 November 1956; (production IIIC) 9 October 1960; (prototype 5) 19 May 1967; (Belgian-assembled 5BA) May 1970.

By far the most commercially successful fighter ever built in Western Europe, the tailless delta Mirage has had little local competition, but has had to contend on the world market with the F-104 and F-5. It had the advantage of proven combat success in 1967 with Israel, the first export customer, and this catapulted it into the limelight and brought sales of 1,410 to 20 different air forces.

The initial Mirage IIIC, now withdrawn from l'Armée de l'Air but still operating in South Africa, has an early Cyrano radar giving limited all-weather and night interception capability. Original armament comprised the Matra R530 missile, with IR or radar homing head, and an alternative of two 30mm guns or a booster rocket pack whose tankage occupied the gun ammunition bay. This rocket is still available, but with the advent of more powerful Atar engines has not been adopted by other customers.

Most of today's aircraft are variants either of the IIIE, a slightly lengthened fighter-bomber with radar and more comprehensive navigation and weapon-delivery avionics, or the 5, a simplified model without radar and able to carry additional fuel or bombs within the same gross weight. This has appealed strongly to third-world countries because of its lower price, and if flown in good weather it has few serious limitations apart from the basic ones that afflict all early tailless deltas; the need for a long runway and the inability to make sustained tight turns without speed bleeding off rapidly. The Mirage III was, in fact, planned to have low-pressure tyres and to operate from rough strips, but the actual tyre pressure combined with the extremely high takeoff and landing speed make this a rare occurrence.

Some customers have bought tandem dual trainers, others the IIIR with a camera filled nose (South Africa's R2Z having the uprated 9K50 engine, and several users the chin bulge showing installation of advanced doppler). Chile brought the final production model, the 50.

At the time of writing a customer has yet to emerge for the IIING (Nouvelle Génération) development which adds a

Above. Abu Dhabi's modestly sized air arm required some 32 Mirages in all, including 12 examples of the 5AD model.

Dassault-Breguet Mirage III and 5

fly-by-wire flight control system, wing-root strakes, fixed canards, inertial navigation, HUD, Cyrano IV radar, laser ranger and additional weapon stations to take advantage of the increased max weight of 32,400lb (14,700kg). Some customers, such as Peru, have updated their Mirages using Dassault-Breguet kits for a HUD, inertial navigation system, laser ranger and Magic AAMs, and the update market for Mirage deltas is now a major one.

The Mirage III/5 story is far from over however. In Switzerland and in France, canard foreplanes are being fitted to add more manoeuvrability in combat. A modification programme is underway on South African Mirage IIIs, which are being completely rebuilt as Atlas Aircraft Cheetahs. These are similar to Israel's Kfir TC7, and as well as canards and dogtooth wings they have revised avionics and weapons.

Right: Nose of the Mirage 5 fitted with small Aida radar.

Right: Nose of the Mirage 5 with no sensors and metal skin.

Right: Nose of the Mirage 5D tandem-seat dual trainer.

Right: Nose of the Mirage 5MBA as used by the Belgian AF.

Above: Comparative noses of the Mirage IIIC (upper) and Mirage IIIE. The latter has a longer fuselage (note engine inlet position) and doppler radar bulge.

Right: Plan view of the EC2/13 aircraft showing weapons.

Below: The Mirage 5F is the Armée de l'Air version of the no-radar Mirage 5. This one flies with EC2/13 "Alpes".

MODERN ATTACK AIRCRAFT

Dassault-Breguet Super Etendard

Origin: Avions Marcel Dassault-Breguet Aviation, France.
Engine: 11,265lb (5,110kg) thrust SNECMA Atar 8K-50 turbojet.
Dimensions: Span 31ft 5.75in (9.6m); length 46ft 11.5in (14.31m); height 12ft 8in (3.85m); wing area 305.7sq ft (28.4m²).
Weights: Empty 14,220lb (6,450kg); loaded 25,350lb (11,500kg).
Performance: Max speed 745mph (1,200km/h) at sea level, Mach 1 at altitude; initial climb 24,600ft (7,500m)/min; service ceiling 45,000ft (13,700m) radius (hi-lo-hi, one AM 39, one tank) 403 miles (650km).
Armament: Two 30mm DEFA cannon, each with 125 rounds; five pylons for weapon load with full internal fuel of 4,630lb (2,100kg); one AM 39 Exocet can be carried (right wing) with one tank (left).
History: First flight (converted Etendard) 28 October 1974; first delivery, late 1977.

The French Aéronavale still uses the original Etendard IVM attack aircraft and IVP photo-reconnaissance machine, in each case often as a "buddy" air refuelling tanker carrying a hose-reel pod. The replacement for the former in four combat units, as described later, is the Super Etendard. This is a very much updated aircraft, though with the advantage of some commonality with the earlier machine. Though called a strike fighter the Super Etendard has little air-combat capability against enemy high-performance aircraft and is used almost wholly in an air/surface role.

Equipment includes an Agave multi-mode radar which is fully adequate for most attacks on surface ships, a Sagem (Kearfott licence) inertial nav/attack system, BF radar warning system and DB-3141 ECM jammer pod. Free-fall bombs of 250 and 400kg sizes can be carried, but the chief anti-ship weapon is the AM 39 Exocet. Super Etendards of the Argentine Navy destroyed HMS *Sheffield* and the *Atlantic Conveyor* with air-launched examples of these missiles.

Right: Catapulting a Super Etendard from the deck of a French Navy aircraft carrier. Note the nose-high attitude.

Dassault Breguet Super Etendard

The Aéronavale planned to buy 100 Super Etendards but inflation reduced the total to 71 in 1978-82. These equip Flottilles 11F and 14F at Landivisiau, 17F at Hyères and 12F at Landivisiau, the latter in the interception mission augmenting the Mach 2 Crusader. The IVP remains in use, but a reconnaissance version of the Super has long been projected. Super Etendard flottiles go to sea aboard the small and aged *Clémenceau* and *Foch*, to replace which two 33,000-tonne nuclear carriers are planned for the end of the century, the keel for the first, *Charles de Gaulle,* being due to be laid in 1986. By this time, however, the basic obsolescence of the Super Etendard will probably have begun to show, and it is hoped to replace it by a carrier-based version of the proposed ACX.

In 1982 Iraq tried to purchase Super Etendards armed with AM 39 missiles to bolster its capability against oil terminals in the war against Iran, but in the event Iraq managed to obtain Exocets for launching from Mirage F1s and Pumas.

In 1985 Dassault announced that it would restart production upon receipt of orders for "about 40", but despite exhibiting an aircraft reconfigured for use from land airfields this came to nothing. In 1987 Dassault tried to get licence manufacture started in Indonesia. Meanwhile Dassault expects to enhance the surviving Aéronavale aircraft from 1991 with the ASMP cruise missile, Anemone radar and upgraded avionics and displays.

Left: Looking up at a Super Etendard armed as in the side view. The perforated air brakes under the belly are prominent.

Below: Side elevation of the 62nd production aircraft. It carries the maximum anti-ship load comprising an AM39 Exocet, two Magic air-to-air missiles and a drop tank.

33

MODERN ATTACK AIRCRAFT

Dassault-Breguet/ Dornier Alpha Jet

Origin: Jointly Dassault-Breguet, France, and Dornier GmbH, W. Germany, with assembly in France (previously at each company); co-production by Egyptian government Factory 36, Helwan.
Engines: Two 2,976lb (1,350kg) thrust SNECMA/Turboméca Larzac C5 turbofans; (NGEA) 3,175lb (1,440kg) Larzac C20.
Dimensions: Span 20ft 10¾in (9.11m); length (excluding any probe) 40ft 3¾in (12.29m); height 13ft 9in 64.2m); wing area 188.4sq ft (17.5m²).
Weights: Empty (trainer) 7,374lb (3,345kg); loaded (clean) 11,023lb (5,000kg) (max) 16,535lb (7,500kg).
Performance: Max speed (clean) 576mph (927km/h) at sea level, 560mph (900km/h) (Mach 0.85) at altitude; climb to 39,370ft (12,000m), less than 10min; service ceiling 48,000ft (14,630m); typical mission endurance 2hr 30min; ferry range with two external tanks 1,827 miles (2,940km).
Armament: Optional for weapon training or combat missions, detachable belly fairing housing one 30mm DEFA or 27mm Mauser cannon, with 125 rounds; same centreline hardpoint and either one or two under each wing (to max of five) canbe provided with pylons for max external load of 5,511lb (2,500kg), made up of tanks, weapons, reconnaissance pod, ECM or other devices.
History: First flight 26 October 1973; first production delivery late 1978.

Though France and Britain were already collaborating on a trainer and light attack aircraft, in 1969 France and West Germany announced a collaborative programme for a less-powerful machine in this class, and after an industry competition the Alpha Jet was selected in 1970. Production was seriously delayed, but eventually a multi-national manufacturing group achieved a high rate of output.

The design was specially arranged with a high wing to give plenty of clearance for underwing stores, though this resulted in a narrow main landing gear track with the units folding into the fuselage. The basic Alpha Jet E, for training and light attack, has tandem staggered Martin-Baker seats, those for the Armée de l'Air being Mk 4s usable at zero height but not below 104mph (167km/h) airspeed, although Egypt, Belgium and Qatar have Mk 10 seats with zero/zero capability.

This model serves with the Armée de l'Air (200 total) to equip the entire Groupement-École 314 "Christian Maretel" at Tours, the Patrouille de France aerobatic team at Salon, the Centre d'Entraînement au Vol Sans Visibilité and the 8e Escadre de Transformation at Cazaux. It is also used (33 supplied) by Belgium's 7, 9 and 11 Sqns at St Truiden (St Trond). All these are pure training or display units, but the Federal German Luftwaffe uses a different version in the close-support and reconnaissance roles.

The Alpha Jet A has the Mauser gun, a pointed nose with pitot probe (aircraft length 43ft 5in, 13.23m) and MBB-built Stencel seats instead of Martin-Baker. A total of 153 was supplied to three fighter/bomber wings; JaboG 49 at Fürstenfeldbruck, JaboG 43 at Oldenburg and JaboG 41 at Husum, each with 51 aircraft on strength. They are austerely equipped for attack missions in the European environment, though navigation systems are good and a HUD (head-up display) is provided. The LaCroix BOZ-10 chaff pod has been developed jointly by France and Germany and is expected to appear with these JaboGs. In the recon role a Super Cyclope pod can be carried with optical cameras, IR linescan and a decoy launcher. Combat missions are expected to be strongly support by Awacs (E-3A Sentry) coverage to make up for deficiencies in the Alpha Jet's defensive avionics. The Luftwaffe has 18 Alpha jets in the weapon-training role at Beja, Portugal, the German total being 175.

The Alternative close-support version has inertial navigation, a HUD laser ranger and radar altimeter, and was co-produced at Helwan, Egypt, as the MS2, the original trainer being known as the MS1. Dassault-Breguet has itself developed this model further into the Alpha Jet 2, with the more powerful Larzac C20 engine and enhanced pylon capability for tanks or Magic AAMs. Dassault/Dornier tried without success to sell various upgraded models including the Lancier attack version.

Above: Originally called the Alpha Jet NGEA, the Alpha Jet 2 has uprated engines and MS2 nav/attack system.

Dassault-Breguet/Dornier Alpha Jet

Above: Three Alphas of the Armee de l'Air. Two are from GE314; the middle (118-BT) is from the CEAM test centre at Mont de Marsan.

Right: Looking up at a bomb-laden Luftwaffe Alpha. Called the Close-support version, its attack potential is limited.

Above: The unusual "chisel nose" of the Alternative close-support version used by Egypt's Air Force as the MS2. This nose houses a laser ranger behind an optically flat glass panel.

Below: The Luftwaffe's Alpha Jets are numbered 40+01 to 41+75. This one is from JBG.43 at Oldenburg.

35

MODERN ATTACK AIRCRAFT

Fairchild Republic A-10A Thunderbolt II

Origin: Fairchild Republic Co., USA.
Engines: Two 9,065lb (4,112kg) thrust General Electric TF34-100 turbofans.
Dimensions: Span 57ft 6in (17.53m); length 53ft 4in (16.26m); height 14ft 8in (4.47m); wing area 506sq ft (47m²).
Weights: Empty 21,519lb (9,761kg); forward airstrip weight (no fuel but four Mk 82 bombs and 750 rounds) 32,730lb (14,846kg); max 50,000lb (22,680kg).
Performance: Max speed (max weight) 423mph (681km/h); cruising speed at sea level 345mph (555km/h); stabilized speed below 8,000ft (2,440m) in 45° dive at weight 35,125lb (15,932kg), 299mph (481km/h); max climb at basic design weight of 31,790lb (14,420kg), 6,000ft (1,828m)/min; service ceiling not stated; take off run to 50ft (15m) at max weight 4,000ft (1,220m); operating radius in CAS mission with 1.8h loiter and reserves 288 miles (463km); radius for single deep strike penetration 620 miles (1,000km); ferry range with allowances 2,542 miles (4,091km).
Armament: One GAU-8/A Avenger 30mm seven-barrel gun with 1,174 rounds, max ordnance load of 16,000lb (7,257kg) hung on 11 pylons; usual load four Mavericks, four self-defence AIM-9 and ALQ-119 ECM pod.
History: First flight (YA-10A) 10 May 1972; (A-10A) 21 October 1975.

Until 1967 the USAF had never bothered to procure a close-support aircraft, instead flying CAS missions with fighters and attack machines. With the A-10, emphasis was placed on the ability to operate from short unpaved front-line airstrips, to carry an exceptional load of weapons — in particular a very powerful high-velocity gun — and to withstand prolonged exposure to gunfire from the ground. Avionics were left to a minimum, the official description for the fit being "austere", but a few extra items are now being added to the Thunderbolt II.

The original A-10A was a basically simple single-seater, larger than most tactical attack aircraft and carefully designed as a compromise between capability and low cost. As an example of the latter many of the major parts, including flaps, main landing gears and movable tail surfaces, are interchangeable left/right, and systems and engineering features were designed with duplication and redundancy to survive parts being shot away. The unusual engine location minimizes infra-red signature and makes it almost simple to fly with one engine inoperative or even shot off.

Weapon pylons were added from tip to tip, but the chief tank-killing ordnance is the gun, the most powerful (in terms of muzzle horsepower) ever mounted in an aircraft, firing milk-bottle size rounds at rates hydraulically controlled at 2,100 or 4,200 shots/min. The gun is mounted 2° nose-down and offset to the left so that the firing barrel is always on the centreline (the nose landing gear being offset to the right).

The basic aircraft has a HUD (Head-up display), good communications fit and both Tacan and inertial navigation. RHAWS and ECM have been internal from the start, but jammer pods are hung externally.

In 1979 Fairchild flew a company-funded NAW (night/adverse weather) demonstrator with augmented avionics and a rear-cockpit for a WSO seated at a higher level and with good forward view. Both the regular and NAW aircraft carry a Pave Penny laser seeker pod under the nose, vital for laser-guided munitions, and the NAW also had a Ferranti laser ranger, Texas Instruments FLIR (forward-

Below: The Pave Penny laser target designator, hung from the right side of the nose, assists the pilot in locking-on the TV camera installed in the extreme nose of the AGM-65A Maverick.

Fairchild Republic A-10A Thunderbolt II

looking infra-red), GE low-light TV and many other items including a Westinghouse multi-mode radar with WSO display. It is probable that A-10As will be brought at least close to the NAW standard, with the LANTIRN pod, though the two-seat NAW itself was never funded. A-10A funding was abruptly terminated in 1982 at a total of 707 aircraft (not including six for RDT&E [research, development, test and evaluation], the last one rolling off the Maryland assembly lines in 1983.

In service with the USAF, AFRes and ANG the A-10A has proved generally popular and unquestionably effective with many weapons. Serviceability and manpower burden have been as predicted, and the only cause for worry is the sustained attrition rate, which is rather higher than normal, caused by hitting the ground during operations at low level. Since late 1987 a total of 26 have been serving as OA-10As in the FAC, SAR, escort and reconnaissance roles.

Above: A four-ship formation of "Warthogs" fly in line astern behind a tanker.

Left: Looking up at an A-10A carrying a varied assortment of external loads. On the fuselage are three crackle-finish GP bombs; on the inboard wing pylons are a KMU-351 Paveway laser-guided bomb (starboard wing) and a GBU-15(V) guided glide bomb (port wing); next come triple AGM-65A Mavericks; finally, under the starboard wing is a Westinghouse ALQ-119(V) ECM jammer pod. For good measure, there is also the GAU-8/A Avenger 30mm gun.

MODERN ATTACK AIRCRAFT

FMA IA 58 and IA 66 Pucará

Origin: Fabrica Militar de Aviones, Argentina.
Engines: Two turboprops, (58) 988shp Turboméca Astazou XVIG, (66) 1,000shp Garrett TPE331-11-601W.
Dimensions: Span 47ft 6.9in (14.5m); length 46ft 9.15in (15.253m); height overall 17ft 7.1in (5.362m); wing area 326.1sq ft (30.3m²).
Weights: Empty (58A) 8,900lb (4,037kg), 66) 8,862lb (4,020kg); max 14,991lb (6,800kg).
Performance: (both) Max speed (9,840ft/3,000m) 310mph (500km/h); econ cruise 267mph (430km/h); takeoff to 50ft (15m) at 12,125lb (5,500kg) 2,313ft (705m); landing from 50ft (15m) 1,978ft (603m); attack radius with max external weapons, 10 per cent reserve fuel (hi-lo-hi) 155 miles (250km), (1,764lb/800kg weapons and external fuel) 559 miles (900km); ferry range 1,890 miles (3,042km).
Armament: Two 20mm Hispano HS804 each with 270 rounds and four 7.62mm FN Browning each with 900 rounds all firing ahead; up to 3,307lb(1,500kg) of wide range of stores carried on three pylons, with individual stores up to 2,205lb (1,000kg), examples including 12 bombs of 276lb (125kg), 12 large napalm tanks, three 1,102lb (500kg) DA bombs, seven 19×2.75in (70mm) rocket pods or a cannon pod and two 72.5gal (330lit) drop tanks.
History: First flight (prototype) 20 August 1969, (58A) 8 November 1974, (66) late 1980.

The Pucará, named after an early hilltop type of stone fortress, was influenced by the US interest in light turboprop Co-In aircraft in the early 1960s. Intended for use against unsophisticated forces, and in fact ordered by the FAA (Argentine Air Force) for suppressing internal disorders, it was planned to have considerable firepower yet operate from austere airstrips with the minimum of ground support.

Features include pilot and copilot in staggered Martin-Baker "zero/zero" seats, carefully disposed armour and equipment for operation by night but not in adverse weather. There is good avionic provision for communications and navigation, and ILS is standard, but weapon aiming is visual. Weather radar is an option.

In the South Atlantic war in spring 1982 about two dozen Pucarás were present in the Falklands, being able to use various airstrips throughout the islands. Despite their good weapon load and inflight agility the island-based machines accomplished little beyond shooting down a British Army Scout AH.1 on 28 May. None returned to Argentina; six were brought to Britain and one was carefully evaluated at Boscombe Down.

FMA had hoped to find a wide export market, but apart from batches of 60 and 48 for the FAA the only other sale until 1988 was six to the air force of Uruguay. Production was continued, however, and eventually ceased in 1986 with a reported total of 23 unsold. Most of the missions flown over the Falklands were by single pilots without backseaters, and FMA tested an IA 66 single-seat version, as well as another single-seat variant designated IA 58C Pucará Charlie. The IA 66 was evaluated by Libya but no sale resulted. In late 1988 however it was announced in Buenos Aires that 50 standard IA 58As had been sold to Egypt, in a barter deal for oil. Some of these must be supplied from FAA stocks.

Left: A 1974 picture of the first production Pucará before delivery. Most later aircraft are similar.

FMA IA 58 and IA 66 Pucará

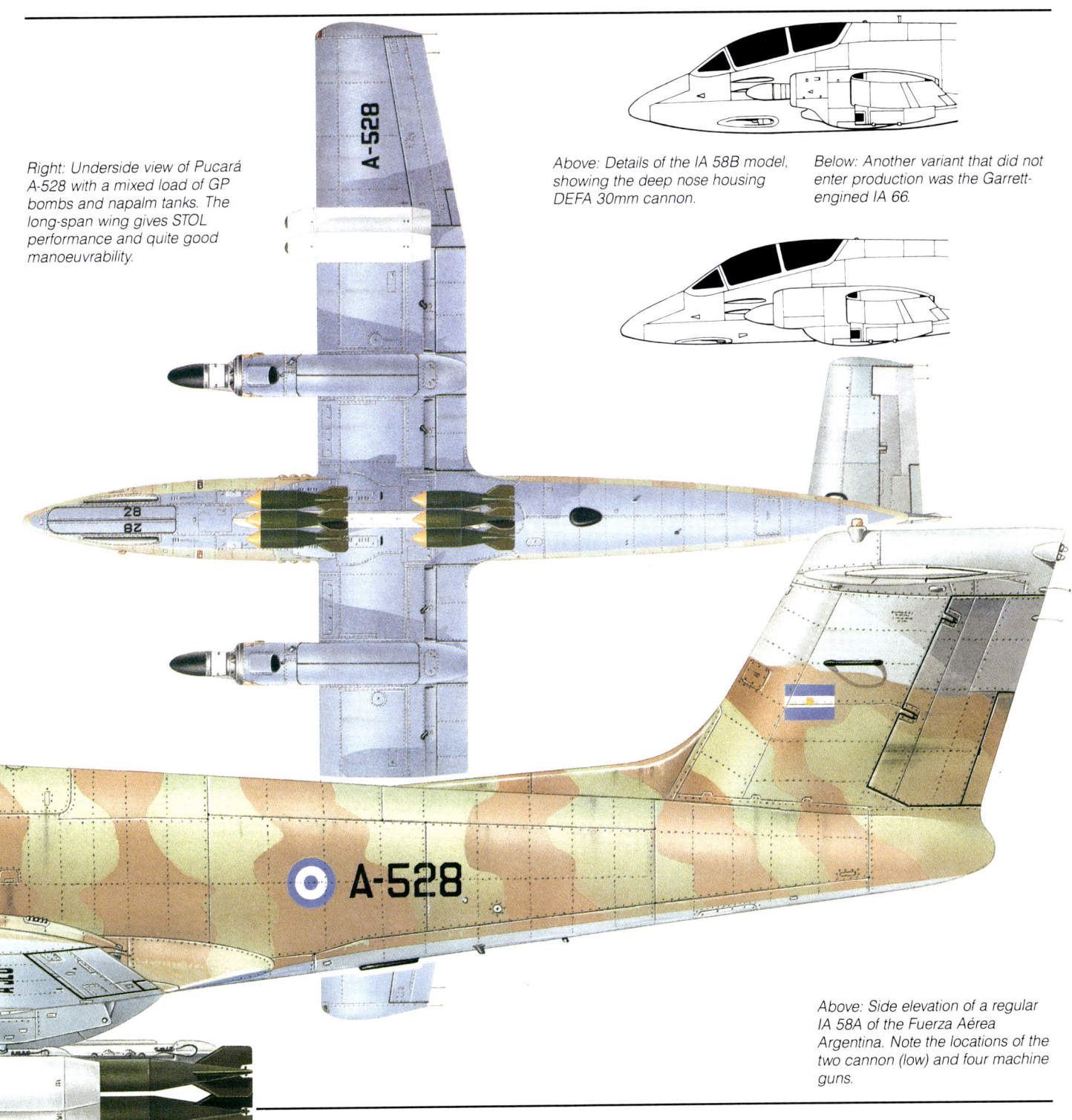

Right: Underside view of Pucará A-528 with a mixed load of GP bombs and napalm tanks. The long-span wing gives STOL performance and quite good manoeuvrability.

Above: Details of the IA 58B model, showing the deep nose housing DEFA 30mm cannon.

Below: Another variant that did not enter production was the Garrett-engined IA 66.

Above: Side elevation of a regular IA 58A of the Fuerza Aérea Argentina. Note the locations of the two cannon (low) and four machine guns.

MODERN ATTACK AIRCRAFT

General Dynamics F-111

Origin: General Dynamics Corporation, USA.
Engines: Two Pratt & Whitney TF30 afterburning turbofans, as follows, (A,C) 18,500lb (8,390kg) TF30-3, (D,E) 19,600lb (8,891kg) TF30-9, (FB) 20,350lb (9,231kg) TF30-7, (F) 25,100lb (11,385kg) TF30-100.
Dimensions: Span (fully spread) (A,D,E,F) 63ft 0in (19.2m), (C,FB) 70ft 0in (21.34m), (fully swept) (A,D,E,F) 31ft 11.5in (9.74m), (C,FB) 33ft 11in (10.34m); length 73ft 6in (22.4m), wing area (A,D,E,F, gross,16°) 525sq ft (48.77m²).
Weights: Empty (A) 46,172lb (20,943kg), (C) 47,300lb (21,455kg), (D) 49,090lb (22,267kg), (E) about 47,000lb (21,319kg), (F) 47,481lb (21,537kg), (FB) close to 50,000lb (22,680kg); loaded (A) 91,500lb (41,500kg), (D,E) 92,500lb (41,954kg), (C,F) 100,000lb (45,360kg), (FB) 114,300lb (51,846kg).
Performance: Max speed at 36,000ft (11,000m), clean and with max afterburner, (A,C,D,E) Mach 2.2, 1,450mph (2,335km/h), (FB) Mach 2, 1,320mph (2,124km/h), (F) Mach 2.5, 1,653mph (2,660km/h); cruising speed, penetration, 571mph (919km/h); range with max internal fuel (A,D) 3,165 miles (5,093km), (F) 2,925 miles (4,707km).
Armament: Internal weapon bay for two B43 bombs or (D,F) one B43 and one M61 gun; three pylons under each wing (four inboard swivelling with wing, outers being fixed and usable only at 16° otherwise being jettisoned) for max external load 31,500lb (14,288kg), (FB only) provision for up to six SRAM, two internal.
History: First flight 21 December 1964; service delivery (A) June 1967.

Basic features of the F-111 include a variable-sweep "swing wing" (the first in production in the world) with limits of 16° and 72.5°, with exceptional high-lift devices, side-by-side seating for the pilot and right-seat navigator (usually also a pilot) or (EF) electronic-warfare officer, large main gears with low-pressure tyres for no-flare landings on soft strips (these prevent the carriage of ordnance on fuselage pylons), a small internal weapon bay, very great internal fuel capacity (typically 5,022 US gal, 19,010 litres), and emergency escape by jettisoning the entire crew compartment, which has its own parachutes and can serve as a survival shelter or boat.

General Dynamics cleared the original aircraft for service in 2½ years, and built 141 of this F-111A version, which equips the 366th TFW at Mountain Home AFB, Idaho (others have been converted into the EF-111A). It is planned to update the A by fitting a digital computer to the original analog-type AJQ-20A nav/bomb system, together with the Air Force standard INS and a new control/display set. The F-111E has larger inlet ducts and engines of slightly greater power — 94 were delivered and survivors equip the 20th TFW at Upper Heyford, England. These will get the same updates as the original F-111A derivative.

Next came the F-111D, which at great cost was fitted with a different avionic system including the APQ-30 attack radar, APN-189 doppler and HUDs for both crew-members. This aircraft has never realized its capabilities, though it remains a major advance on the A and E. The 96 built equip the 27th TFW at Cannon AFB, New Mexico.

The F-111F is the best of all tactical versions, because Pratt & Whitney produced a more powerful TF30 giving enhanced life with fewer problems. With greater performance than other models, the F could double in an air-control role though it has no weapons for this role except the gun and AIM-9. The 106 examples built served at Mountain Home until transfer to the 48th TFW in England, at Lakenheath.

The most important post-delivery modification has been the conversion of the F force to use the Pave Tack pod, normally stowed in the weapon bay but rotated out on a cradle for use. This complex package provides a day/night all-weather capability to acquire, track, designate and hit surface targets using EO, IR or laser guided weapons. The first squadron to convert was the 48th TFW's 494th TFS, in September 1981. Their operations officer said: "Important targets that once required several aircraft can now be disabled with a single Pave Tack aircraft; the radar tells the pod where to look, and the laser allows us to put the weapon precisely on target."

The long-span FB-111A was bought to replace the B-58 and early models of B-52 in SAC, though the rising price resulted in a cut in procurement from 210 to 76, entering service in

Below: Side elevation of an F-111F of the USAF's 48th Tactical Fighter Wing at RAF Lakenheath. It is fitted with a Pave Tack pod (see text above).

General Dynamics F-111

October 1969. It has so-called Mk IIB avionics, derived from those of the D but configured for SAC missions using nuclear bombs or SRAMs. With strengthened structure and landing gear the FB equips SAC's 380th BW at Plattsburgh AFB, NY, and the 509th at Pease, New Hampshire. As the Northrop B-2 enters service the FBs will be updated to F-111G standard and moved to Europe.

The RAAF purchased 24 F-111Cs in 1963, and finally received them in 1973. These have the long-span wing and strengthened landing gear of the FB, but are basically otherwise F-111As. The RAAF decided to have its own reconnaissance pallet developed by GD, with cameras, IR linescan, TV, optical sights and sensor controls and displays in the right-hand cockpit. Four modified aircraft serve with RAAF No 6 Sqn at Amberley, the other F-111 unit being No.1 Sqn at the same base. Four F-111Cs lost have been replaced by F-111As bought second-hand. The RAAF has evaluated various sensors and missiles for use in the maritime and anti-ship role.

Today GD is updating the avionics of all 381 aircraft in the USAF inventory, under a basic $1.1 billion six-year contract. GE will provide new attack radars, TI new TFRs and other suppliers new (but mainly off-the-shelf) navigation, communications, IFF and EW subsystems.

Far right: Some idea of the weapons payload is provided by an F-111A carrying 24 Mk.82 general purpose bombs.

Below: An underside view of an F-111F, configured with Pave Tack and carrying four Paveway smart bombs.

Above: F-111 wing sweep can vary from 16 to 72.5 deg.

41

MODERN ATTACK AIRCRAFT

Grumman A-6 Intruder

Origin: Grumman Corporation, USA.
Engines: Two 9,300lb (4,218kg) thrust Pratt & Whitney J52-8A turbojets.
Dimensions: Span 53ft (16.15m); length 54ft 7in (16.64m); height (KA-6D) 15ft 7in (4.75m); (A-6E) 16ft 3in (4.95m); wing area 528.9sq ft (49.1m²).
Weights: Empty (A-6E) 25,630lb (11,625kg); max loaded (AE-6) 60,400lb (27,397kg).
Performance: Max speed (A-6E) 648mph (1,043km/h) at sea level; initial climb (A-6E, clean) 8,600ft (2,621m)/min; service ceiling (A-6E) 44,600ft (13,595m), range with full combat load (A-6E) 1,077 miles (1,733km); ferry range with external fuel in jettisonable auxiliary tanks is of the order of 3,100 miles (4,890km).
Armament: Five stores locations each rated at 3,600lb (1,633kg) with max total load of 15,000lb (6,804kg); typical load thirty 500lb (227kg) bombs. KA-6D in-flight refuelling tanker derivative also has limited attack capability.
History: First flight (YA2F-1) 19 April 1960; service acceptance of A-6A 1 February 1963; first flight (KA-6D) 23 May 1966; (A-6E) 27 February 1970. Improved A-6F version flown for the first time on 25 August 1987 but cancelled when Congress deleted funding.

Despite its seemingly outdated concept, the A-6 Intruder will remain in low-rate production throughout the foreseeable future as the standard equipment of all the medium attack squadrons of the US Navy and Marine Corps. The design was formulated during the later part of the Korean war, in 1953, when the need for a truly all-weather attack aircraft was first recognized. After much refinement of the requirement an industry competition was held in 1957, Grumman's G-128 design being chosen late in that year.

Basic characteristics of all aircraft of the family include a conventional long-span wing with almost full-span flaps on both the leading and trailing edges. Ahead of the trailing-edge flaps are "flaperons" used as lift spoilers and ailerons, while the tips contain split airbrakes which are fully opened on each carrier landing. Plain turbojets were used, and these have remained in all successive production versions. The nose is occupied by a giant radar array, with a fixed inflight-refuelling probe in front of the side-by-side cockpit with Martin-Baker seats (slightly inclined and staggered) which can be tilted back to reduce fatigue.

Grumman delivered 482 of the original A-6A model, ending in December 1969, and 62 of these were converted into KA-6D air-refuelling tankers which can transfer over 21,000lb (9,526kg) of fuel through its hosereel. This remains the standard tanker of the 14 carrier air wings, with limited attack capability and equipment for use as an air/sea rescue control platform. The A-6A, B and C are no longer in use, the standard attack model being the A-6E. This has a new radar, the Norden APQ-148, as well as an IBM/Fairchild computer-based attack and weapon-delivery system. In 1974 an A-6E was fitted with the TRAM (target recognition and attack multisensor) package, comprising a stabilized chin turret containing a FLIR and a laser interlinked with the radar for detection, identification and weapon-guidance at greater ranges in adverse conditions. Other updates with TRAM include the Litton ASN-92 CAINS (carrier aircraft inertial navigation system), a new CNI suite and automatic carrier landing.

Originally it was planned to deploy a force of 318 A-6Es, but the total went well beyond this. Grumman converted a total of 240 A-6As and has so far added a further 195 newly built E-versions. By 1988 all had been given the complete TRAM conversion, which since 1981 has also equipped Intruders to launch up to four AGM-84 Harpoon anti-ship cruise missiles.

Nevertheless, these updates were never intended to prolong the life of the A-6E beyond 1990, and in 1984 Grumman was awarded a contract to plan a much more extensive upgrade programme. The result was the A-6F, the first of which flew on 25 August 1987. Major changes included a switch to the lighter, more powerful and much more fuel-efficient General

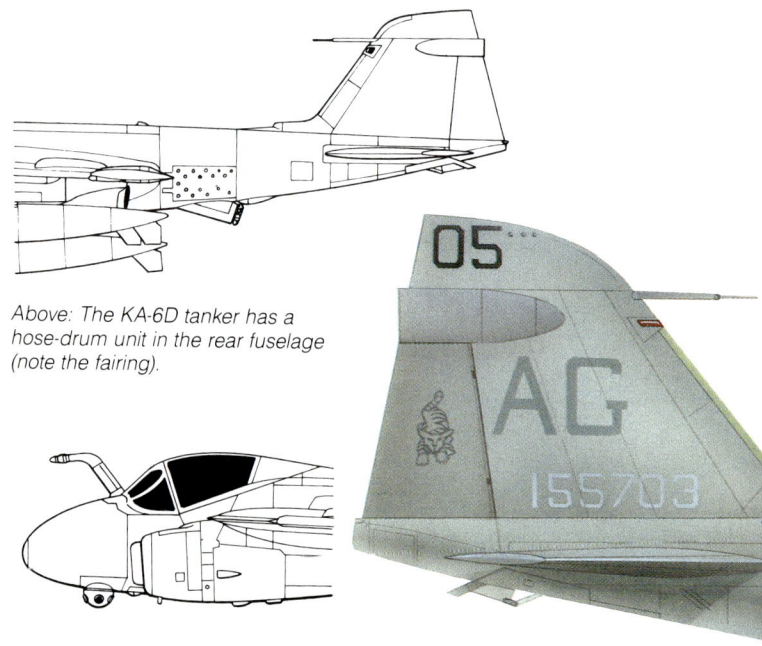

Above: The KA-6D tanker has a hose-drum unit in the rear fuselage (note the fairing).

Above: All A-6Es have a fixed in-flight refuelling probe above the nose; some have a TRAM turret below.

Right: A-6E BuNo 155703 seen as aircraft Modex 505 of VA-65 "Tigers" attack squadron.

Grumman A-6 Intruder

Electric F404 engine, a substantially revised airframe, new systems and, most important of all, a completely new suite of avionics and cockpit displays. Norden developed the APQ-173 multimode radar, and there were to be new computers, radio, navaids, HUD, weapon aiming systems and electronic warfare systems. Provision was to be made for many new weapons including Maverick, HARM and Amraam. In 1988 Congress deleted funding for the A-6F, but it is possible that the avionic upgrades may still be incorporated in existing aircraft.

In an unrelated programme Boeing is rewinging up to 102 A-6Es with a new graphite (carbonfibre) wing. This will eliminate existing fatigue caused by sustained operation at high weights. Boeing has options for 336 wing sets.

Left: Marine Corps A-6Es of VMA (AW) -332 each carry four underwing fuel tanks during a long-range ferry flight.

Below: This underside view shows an A-6E fitted with a TRAM turret and armed with triple AGM-65F Mavericks.

43

MODERN ATTACK AIRCRAFT

SOKO/CNIAR IAR 93 Orao

Origin: Joint programme by CNIAR, Romania, and SOKO, Yugoslavia.
Engines: Two Rolls-Royce Viper turbojets licence-built by Turbomecanica of Romania and ORAO of Yugoslavia, (development aircraft and 93A) 4,000lb (1,814kg) thrust Mk 632-41R, (production Orao and 93B) 5,000lb (2,268kg) Mk 633-47 with afterburners.
Dimensions: Span 31ft 6.7in (9.62m); length (single-seat, inc probe) 48ft 10.6in (14.9m), (two-seat, inc probe) 52ft 2in (15.9m); height overall 14ft 7.2in (4.45m); wing area 279.86sq ft (26.0m²).
Weights: Empty (single-seat 93A) 13,558lb (6,150kg), (93B) 12,566lb (5,700kg); loaded (clean) (A) 19,458lb (8,826kg), (B) 18,953lb (8,597kg); max (A) 22,765lb (10,326kg), (B) 24,692lb (11,200kg).
Performance: Max speed at SL (A) 665mph (1,070km/h), (B) 721mph (1,160km/h); service ceiling (A) 34,450ft (10,500m); (B) 44,300ft (13,500m); takeoff/landing over 50ft (15m) (A) 5,250ft (1,600m); mission radius (A, max external weapons) (lo-lo-lo) 186 miles (300km), (hi-lo-lo) 224 miles (360km).
Armament: Two internal GSh-23 twin-barrel 23mm guns each with 200 rounds; five pylons, centreline rated 1,102lb (500kg), inners 992lb (450kg) and outers 551lb (250kg), for total load of 3,307lb (1,500kg).
History: First flight 31 October 1974, (B) late 1983.

By far the biggest aircraft project ever undertaken in any Balkan country, the YuRom (so called from its participating countries) has been delayed by the decision to power it with a locally developed afterburning version of the Viper turbojet, and also by protracted arguments on precisely what the two air forces (one of them a member of the Warsaw Pact) really want. The design crystallized as a kind of lower powered Jaguar, without great pretentions as an air-superiority fighter but capable of giving a good account of itself in front-line tactical missions in support of a land battle.

From the start the project has been split 50/50 between the two countries (though the fact that a prototype made its first flight in each country within 20 minutes of each other on the same day is said to have been coincidental). There is no duplication, CNIAR's plant at Craiova making the forward and centre fuselage and horizontal tail and SOKO's factory at Mostar the remainder. Thus the airframe is common to both nations, and so is the Messier-Hispano-Bugatti landing gear based on that of the Jaguar, as well as the Martin-Baker 10J seats and a few other items. Yet each country has elected to go ahead with quite different systems and equipment, so that what finally emerge are two quite different aircraft, without even considering avionics and weapons! To the Romanians it is the CNIAR 93 while the Yugoslavs call it the SOKO Orao (Eagle).

Basic features include large slotted flaps, outboard powered ailerons, powered full-span slats, and powered rudder slab tailplanes, the latter having anti-flutter tip masses on all aircraft seen by early 1984 but intended to be eliminated from production machines. Large perforated airbrakes are hinged ahead of the main gears beneath the bays occupied by the guns, which in turn are immediately below the engine inlet ducts which are very simple. A braking parachute is housed beneath the rudder. The production machine has a large Lerx (leading-edge root extension) as well as a narrow strake along each side of the nose to improve airflow in tight turns (7g is permissible).

The cockpit is pressurized and has an upward-opening canopy, and that of the Orao would be instantly familiar to an RAF Jaguar pilot; the IAR 93B has a more Soviet type avionic fit, including comprehensive EW systems. No radar has been requested, but various weapons-aiming systems are being studied apart from the current Ferranti gyro sight.

An afterburning aircraft at last got into the air in the final days of 1983, and this enhances performance at some cost in greater fuel burn. It is expected that a proportion of production machines will be two-seaters, which have dual pilot cockpits, the front cockpit moved slightly forward and the rear cockpit in place of a fuselage fuel cell giving reduced endurance. The production aircraft is also expected to have

SOKO/CNIAR IAR 93 Orao

integral-tank wings, replacing small separate bladder cells in aircraft flying before 1984.

It is possible that after so much passage of time the original national requirements have changed, and the Yugoslavs are certainly keeping a very low profile on this programme, though Romania has ordered 20 IAR 93As and 165 IAR 93Bs for inventory service and these were expected to be delivered from late 1984. Totals are liable to vary, however.

Above: One of the Yugoslavian Air Force's SOKO Oraos is shown with a typical ordnance load underwing as well as a belly fuel tank.

Below: The Orao's similarity to the Anglo-French Jaguar is evident in this side profile of a bomb-laden example featuring Yugoslav Air Force national insignia.

Below: An early example of the SOKO Orao is depicted in landing configuration with the forward fuselage air brakes deployed.

45

MODERN ATTACK AIRCRAFT

Lockheed F-117A

Origin: United States.
Engines: Two modified General Electric F404-400D turbofans each rated at about 10,800lb (4,899kg) thrust.
Dimensions: Not disclosed, but span about 45ft (13.7m) and length about 25ft (7.6m); wing area about 350ft² (32.5m²).
Weights: Not disclosed, but empty probably about 20,000lb (9t) and maximum probably about 40,000lb (18t).
Performance: Not disclosed, but max speed at low level probably about 700mph (1,127km/h); one estimate of max cruising speed is 645mph (1,038km/h); one estimate of combat range is 460 miles (741km).
Armament: Internal bay can carry up to 4,400lb (2t) of weapons as an alternative to reconnaissance sensors; weapons are said to include various types of AGM-65 Maverick air/surface missile and could include AGM-88 HARM and stand-off or dispenser type weapons. No air combat capability has been surmised.
History: For background see text, first flight of F-117 June 1981; service delivery October 1983.

Remarkably, while the rollout of the much later Northrop B-2 "stealth" bomber was a public occasion, this much earlier and smaller "stealth" aircraft has never been officially acknowledged by the USAF except for the release of a single black and white photograph of poor quality in November 1988. Two weeks previously, the US Secretary of Defense, Frank Carlucci, said "Not since the Manhattan Project have we seen a program cloaked in such secrecy and with such enormous potential to guarantee the security of our nation". The Manhattan Project was the development of the first nuclear weapons in World War II.

Predictably, the team entrusted with the main development of LO (low observables) or "stealth" aircraft was Lockheed's famed Skunk Works, or Advanced Development Projects facility, headed by Ben Rich. Today, this is part of Lockheed Aeronautical Systems Co. The work began "in house" by the USAF, which took a Wittman Tailwind lightplane and modified it to reduce noise, IR (infra-red or heat) signature and RCS (radar cross section). Next, Lockheed built a batch of XST (experimental stealth technology) research/demo aircraft, each as nearly as possible a scaled-down version of the proposed production aircraft. Powered by two 2,800lb (1,270kg) thrust GE CJ610 turbojets, the first XST flew in 1977. Results were very encouraging, though two XSTs are thought to have crashed.

The full-scale CSIRS (covert survivable in-weather recon/strike), now announced as having the designation F-117A, first flew in June 1981. The single pilot sits high in a nose cockpit with surprisingly large glass windows set at carefully chosen angles for minimal reflection of the Sun or of radar waves. The aircraft is nearly all-wing, with a stumpy fuselage blended in between the two above-wing engines. The latter have inlets arranged to "capture" radar energy and also minimise IR and noise. The unaugmented engines discharge through very unconventional nozzles at the back which surround the core jet with cool air and as far as possible shroud it with structure. Above the large nozzles are twin butterfly tails, which appear to be of the all-moving type, and there are control surfaces along the trailing edge of the delta wing. In the nose are what resemble pitot tubes.

Lockheed has reportedly delivered 59 CSIRS aircraft, the operating unit being the 4450th Tactical Group (originally Tactical Test Group). The unit HQ is at Nellis AFB, Nevada, but the F-117As operate from the remote Tonopah AFS.

The F-117A's mission is to penetrate heavily defended enemy airspace and bring back reconnaissance imagery and/or carry out precision attacks on surface targets. It is widely reported to be "almost undetectable except at extremely close range". One of the design requirements is said to have been the ability of the aircraft to be airlifted in a C-5 Galaxy, which would require quickly removable or folding wings and a span across the engines not exceeding 19ft (5.79m). Of course, the F-117A is coated with special materials to minimise RCS and visible contrast and it emits little or no detectable radiation in defended areas.

Lockheed F-117A

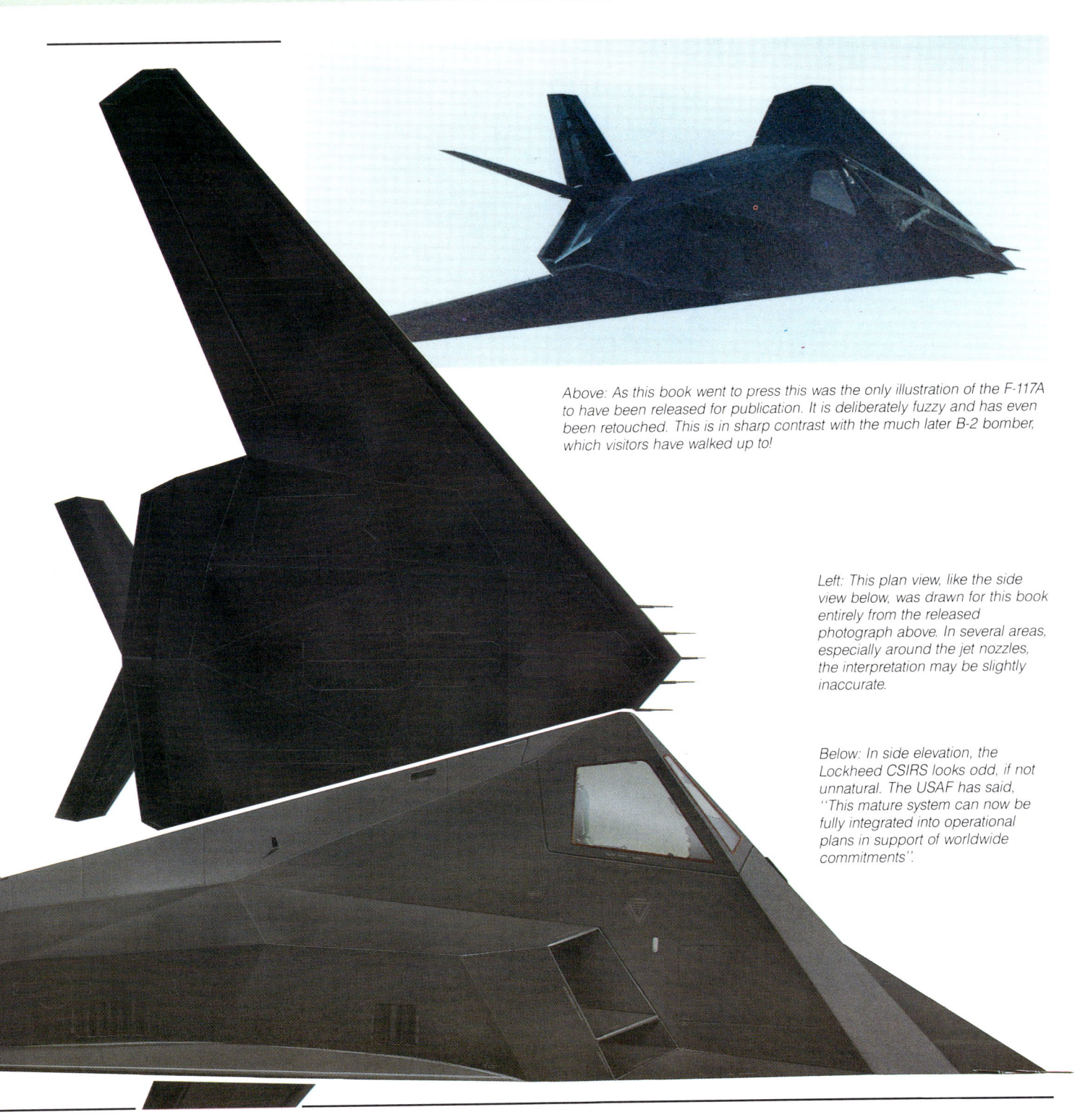

Above: As this book went to press this was the only illustration of the F-117A to have been released for publication. It is deliberately fuzzy and has even been retouched. This is in sharp contrast with the much later B-2 bomber, which visitors have walked up to!

Left: This plan view, like the side view below, was drawn for this book entirely from the released photograph above. In several areas, especially around the jet nozzles, the interpretation may be slightly inaccurate.

Below: In side elevation, the Lockheed CSIRS looks odd, if not unnatural. The USAF has said, "This mature system can now be fully integrated into operational plans in support of worldwide commitments".

MODERN ATTACK AIRCRAFT

McDonnell Douglas A-4 Skyhawk

Origin: Douglas Aircraft Company, USA.
Engine: (E, J) One 8,500lb (3,856kg) Pratt & Whitney J52-6 turbojet; (F, G, H, K) 9,300lb (4,218kg) J52-8A; (M, N, Y) 11,200lb (5,080kg) J52-408A.
Dimensions: Span 27ft 6in (8.38m); length (E, F, G, H, K, L, P, Q, S) 40ft 1.5in (12.22m), (M, N, Y) 40ft 3.2in (12.27m), (OA, and TA, excluding probe) 42ft 7.25in (12.98m); height 15ft (4.57m), (TA series 15ft 3in); wing area 250sq ft (24.17m²).
Weights: Empty (E) 9,284lb, (4,211kg) (typical single-seat, eg Y) 10,465lb (4,747kg), (TA-4F) 10,602lb (4,809kg); max (shipboard) 24,500lb (11,113kg); (land-based) 27,420lb (12,437kg).
Performance: Max speed (clean) (E) 685mph (1,102km/h), (Y) 670mph (1,078km/h). (TA-4F) 675mph (1,086km/h); max speed (4,000lb/1,814kg bomb load) (Y) 645mph (1,038km/h); initial climb (Y) 8,440ft (2,572m)/min; service ceiling about 49,000ft (14,935m); range (clean, or with 4,000lb weapons and max fuel, late versions) about 920 miles (1,480km); max range (Y) 2,055 miles (3,307km).
Armament: Standard on most versions, two 20mm Mk 12 cannon, each with 200 rounds; (H, N, and optional on other export versions) two 30mm DEFA 553, each with 150 rounds, Pylons under fuselage and wings for total ordnance load of (E, F, G, H, K, L, P, Q, S) 8,200lb (3,720kg); (M, N, Y) 9,155lb (4,153kg).
History: First flight (XA4D-1) 22 June 1954; delivery October 1956; (A-4M) April 1970; first TA series (TA-4E) June 1965.

The ultimate expression of designer Ed Heinemann's art in meeting a challenging requirement (for a carrier-based attack aircraft) with an aircraft which weighed just half the suggested figure and flew 100 knots (185km/h) faster, the A-4 remained in production for 26 years, from 1954 to 1979 inclusive. The final total was 2,980, and thanks to continual updating many are in service today, with third-world airpowers taking careful note of each used Skyhawk that comes on to the market.

The US Marine Corps currently operates a large number of A-4s in various roles. The single-seat combat aircraft is the A-4Y, some built new and others reworked A-4Ms with Marconi HUD, an advanced ARBS similar to that of the Harrier II and enhanced EW systems. The OA-4M tandem-seat FAC platform is a rebuild of the TA-4F trainer, and the

Left: Tails of (front) an A-4 with IR-suppressed jetpipe and (rear) an A-4M/N with warning antenna.

Below: Featuring desert camouflage, the first A-4N for Israel carries Bullpup missiles underwing.

Above: All late A-4s have "camel hump" avionics packs. Some also have Hughes ARBS.

Above: Side elevation of an A-4M Skyhawk of USMC light attack squadron VMA-214. In the USMC, the A-4 is being replaced by the AV-8B.

McDonnell Douglas A-4 Skyhawk

the latter together with the simple and agile TA-4J continue as advanced pilot trainers, especially for teaching air combat tactics.

The most important of the export customers was Israel, which purchased 279 single-seaters of various types and 27 two-seaters. Today Israel's IAI is on to good business with its offer of retrofitting A-4s for a of export customers.

The IAI-modified A-4s have an extended nose and a 'saddleback hump' for various new avionic options, extended jetpipe to reduce IR signature, underwing spoilers, steerable nosewheel, dual disc mainwheel brakes, braking parachute, 30mm guns, two extra wing pylons, updated EW and chaff/flare dispensers, a new weapon-delivery avionic system, and complete structural life-extension and rewiring. Argentina continues to be a good Israeli customer, and it was reported in 1984 that IAI had begun to supply three Gabriel III/AS anti-ship missiles for each A-4 then in service with Argentinian combat units.

Another major Skyhawk user is Singapore, whose aircraft include the unique TA-4S trainer version with separate canopies over the staggered tandem cockpits. Since 1985 SAI (Singapore Aircraft Industries) has been engaged in a major programme to rebuild Skyhawks to the A-4S-1 standard. The chief change is a switch to the General Electric F404-100D turbofan engine rated at 11,000lb (4,990kg) thrust. Completely new digital avionics are installed, including a Ferranti nav/attack system and interfaces for Maverick surface-attack missiles. Following prolonged testing of two prototypes SAI is now working on the conversion of about 50 aircraft of the Singapore Air Force.

Above: The separate canopies of Singapore's unique TA-4S are highly distinctive.

Below: Underside view of an A-4M showing triple "slick" Mk.82 bombs, centreline tank and AGM-12 Bullpup ASMs.

MODERN ATTACK AIRCRAFT

McDonnell Douglas F-4 Phantom II

Origin: McDonnell Aircraft Co, USA (F-4EJ by Mitsubishi, Japan).
Engines: (C, D) two 17,000lb (7,711kg) General Electric J79-15 turbojets with afterburner; (E, F, G) 17,900lb (8,120kg) J79-17; (J, N, S) 17,900lb J79-10; (K, M) 20,515lb (9,305kg) Rolls-Royce Spey 202/203 augmented turbofans.
Dimensions: Span 38ft 5in (11.7m); length (C, D, J, N, S) 58ft 3in (17.76m), (E, G, F) 62ft 11in or 63ft (19.2m), (K, M) 57ft 7in (17.55m); height (all) 16ft 3in (4.96m); wing area 530sq ft (49.2m²).
Weights: Empty (C, D, J, N) 28,000lb (12,700kg), (E, F) 29,000lb (13,150kg), (G, K, M) 31,000lb (14,060kg); max (C, D, J, K, M, N) 58,000lb (26,308kg), (E, G, F) 60,630lb (27,502kg).
Performance: Max speed with Sparrow missiles only (low) 910mph (1,464km/h, Mach 1.19) with J79 engines, 920mph with Spey; (high) 1,500mph (2,414km/h, Mach 2.27) with J79, 1,386mph with Spey; initial climb, typically 28,000ft (8,534m)/min with J79, 32,000ft/min with Spey; service ceiling over 60,000ft (19,685m) with J79, 60,000ft with Spey; range on internal fuel (no weapons) about 1,750 miles (2,817km); ferry range with external fuel, typically 2,300 miles (3,700km), (E and variants), 2,600 miles (4,184km).
Armament: Four AIM-7 Sparrow or Sky Flash (later Amraam) air-to-air missiles recessed under fuselage; inner wing pylons can carry two more AIM-7 or four AIM-9 Sidewinder missiles; in addition E versions have 20mm M61 gun, and all versions have four wing pylons for tanks, bombs or other stores to total weight of 16,000lb (7,257kg).
History: First flight (XF4H-1) 27 May 1958; service delivery (F-4A) February 1961 (inventory); first flight (Air Force F-4C) 27 May 1963; (F-4E) 30 June 1967; (F-4G) 1976.

By far the most important fighter in the non-Communist world during the past 20 years, the F-4 has an evergreen quality of sheer capability that from time to time is recognized. There were 5,195 F-4s constructed, far surpassing all other Western fighters since World War II except for the F-84 and F-86 families.

The F-4B for the US Navy introduced blown flaps and leading edges, a broad fuselage with four AIM-7 Sparrows recessed into the underside, wing and centreline pylons for tanks, Sidewinders, bombs or other stores, tremendous internal fuel capacity, tandem seats for pilot and RIO (radar intercept officer) and a powerful Westinghouse radar. This sub-family was continued via the F-4J to the F-4N and F-4S rebuilds with more fuel, revised structures and avionics, slatted wings and tailplanes, and other updates.

The original USAF version was a minimum-change variant, the F-4C of 1963. This proved so satisfactory that the Air Force was allowed to have its own F-4D, with ground attack avionics. This was followed during the Vietnam War by the F-4E with uprated engines, an extra rear-fuselage tank, a new and smaller radar, an M61 gun and, in the course of the production run, leading-edge slats to improve the previously poor agility when heavily laden.

West Germany's Luftwaffe chose a simpler F-4F model without provision for Sparrow or various EW subsystems. Mitsubishi assembled 138 F-4E(J) Phantoms in Japan, with increasing local content. In 1964-5 Britain bought the F-4K (Phantom FG.1) for the Navy and the F-4M (FGR.2) for the RAF. Both were largely redesigned with Spey engines. In low-level use the big fan engines do a good job, and other features include carrier provisions on the FG.1 and on the FGR.2 a Ferranti INS, AWG/11/12 radar fire control, strike camera in one AAM recess and fin-cap RWR.

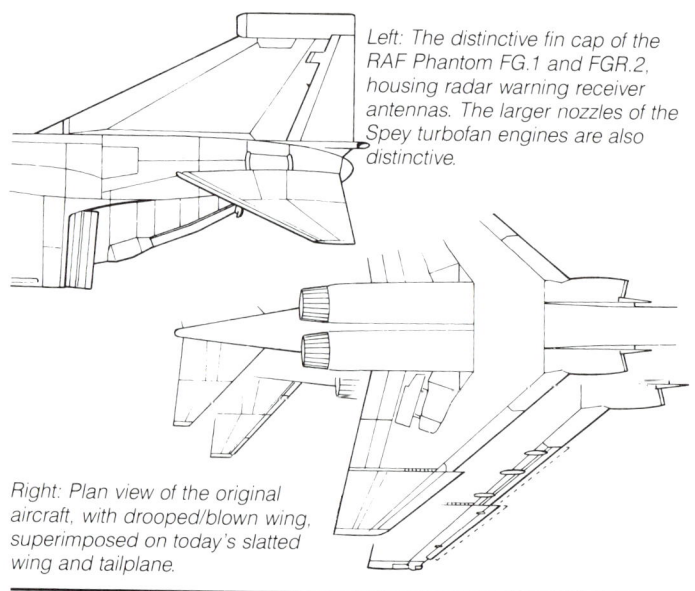

Left: The distinctive fin cap of the RAF Phantom FG.1 and FGR.2, housing radar warning receiver antennas. The larger nozzles of the Spey turbofan engines are also distinctive.

Right: Plan view of the original aircraft, with drooped/blown wing, superimposed on today's slatted wing and tailplane.

50

McDonnell Douglas F-4 Phantom II

To make up for a unit in the Falklands 15 ex-US F-4J fighters have been purchased for service with No. 74 Sqn at Wattisham.

Latest version is the F-4G Advanced Wild Weasel EW platform, whose mission is to sense, locate and destroy hostile ground air-defence emitters. Used only by the USAF, this is a rebuild of late-model F-4E fighters with the APR-38 EW system whose 52 special antennas include large pods facing forwards under the nose and to the rear above the rudder. The system is governed by a Texas Instruments computer with reprogrammable software to keep up to date on hostile emitters.

This Phantom carries such weapons as triplets of the AGM-65 EO-guided Maverick precision attack weapon, Shrike ARM (anti-radar missile) and HARM (high-speed ARM). Like almost all Phantoms the left front fuselage recess often carries an ECM jammer pod (usually an ALQ-119 but more recently the ALQ-131), leaving the other three available for Sparrow AAMs if necessary; or Sidewinders can be carried under the wings.

In 1984 Germany's F-4Fs and Japan's F-4E(J)s were subjects of major update programmes with look-down pulse-doppler radars. Meanwhile, Israel Aircraft Industries hopes to re-engine as many F-4s as possible with the PW1120 engine, rated at 20,620lb (9,353kg) thrust. The first conversion flew in July 1986. This is one stage in the IAI plan for a totally upgraded Phantom 2000.

Left: F-4G Wild Weasels of the 37th TFW carrying a mixture of armament including cluster bomb units, Maverick and anti-radar air-to-surface missiles

Right: The J, K, M and S all have AWG-10 or -11 fire-control, while the F-4E and F have a gun and small radar.

Above: Underside view of an F-4E in the fighter role, carrying four recessed Sparrow AAMs, four Sidewinders, two tanks and gun.

Below: Side view of the same aircraft, which still serves with the 4th TFW at Seymour-Johnson AFB, North Carolina.

MODERN ATTACK AIRCRAFT

McDonnell Douglas F-18 Hornet

Origin: McDonnell Aircraft Company USA; RAAF aircraft assembled by GAF, Australia.
Engines: Two 16,000lb (7,258kg) General Electric F404-400 afterburning turbofans.
Dimensions: Span (with missiles) 40ft 4.75in (12.31m), (without missiles) 37ft 6in (11.42m); length 56ft (17.07m); height 15ft 3.5in (4.66m); wing area 400sq ft (36.16m²).
Weights: Empty 23,050lb (10,455kg); loaded (attack mission) 49,224lb (22,328kg).
Performance: Max speed (clean, at altitude) 1,190mph (1,915km/h, Mach 1.8), (max weight, sea level) subsonic; sustained combat manoeuvre ceiling, 49,000ft (14,935m); combat radius (air-to-air mission, high, no external fuel) 461 miles (741km); ferry range, more than 2,300 miles (3,700km).
Armament: One 20mm M61 gun with 570 rounds in upper part of forward fuselage, nine external weapon stations for max load (catapult launch) of 13,400lb (6,080kg) or (land takeoff) of 17,000lb (7,711kg), including bombs, sensor pods, missiles (including Sparrow) and other stores, with tip-mounted Sidewinders.
History: First flight (YF-17) 9 June 1974, (first of 11 test F-18) 18 November 1978; (production F/A-18) 1980; service entry, 1982.

It is remarkable that this twin-engined machine designed for carrier operation should have won three major export sales almost entirely because of its ability to kill hostile aircraft at stand-off distance using radar-guided AAMs (which with a few trivial changes could be done by its losing rival, the F-16). From the outset in 1974 the Hornet was designed to be equally good at both fighter and attack roles, replacing the F-4 and A-7. The design was derived from the Northrop YF-17, and Northrop is principal subcontractor.

Where the Hornet is unquestionably superior is in the engineering of the aircraft itself, which is probably the best

Below: Side elevation of an F/A-18A Hornet (BuNo 161952) of USMC squadron VMFA-122 "Crusaders". Northrop make the centre and rear fuselage and tail section.

McDonnell Douglas F-18 Hornet

yet achieved in any production combat type, and in particular in the detail design for easy routine maintenance and sustained reliability. Of course, in the low-level attack role it suffers from a wide-span fixed wing giving severe gust response, relatively low maximum speed and lack of terrain-following radar; but with a mission mainly over the sea and a dive on target these shortcomings are less important. Attack radius has also been criticized.

The cockpit is a major "plus" for this aircraft, with Hotas controls (the stick being conventional instead of a sidestick), up-front CNI controls and three excellent MFDs (multifunction displays) which replace virtually all the traditional instruments. This cockpit goes further than anything previously achieved in enabling one man to handle the whole of a defensive or an offensive mission. But this is not to deny that a second crewmember would not ease the workload, especially in hostile airspace, and in 1987 production switched to the F/A-18C with upgraded avionics (for night attack from 1989) and F/A-18D with a fully equipped rear cockpit for a naval flight officer.

There is, of course, a two-seat dual-pilot version for conversion training; this retains weapons capability and the APG-65 radar, but has about 6 per cent less internal fuel. There is also a prototype of a dedicated reconnaissance F/A-18 (RC), testing of which began in 1984. This has a new nose, with the gun and ammunition replaced by a recon package which would normally include optical cameras and/or AAD-5 IR linescan. It is stated that this model could "overnight" be converted into the fighter/attack configuration.

The CF-18 for the Canadian Forces differs in small items such as having a spotlight for visual identification of aircraft at night. Canada has only a small manufacturng offset (Canadair makes nose sections), despite the size of the order: 138, including 24 two-seaters. Deliveries began in October 1982, and in 1988 Canada was trying to buy used F/A-18s to replace losses.

Australia's buy of 57 AF-18As plus 18 TFs, triggered a vast and complex involvement of local industry. The first two TFs were delivered from St Louis in October 1984. The rest are being assembled by Government Aircraft Factories, with major Australian content in 1985-90. Spain bought 72 EF-18A and EF-18B, called C.15 and CE.15 locally.

Left: From this angle, the muzzle of the 20mm gun can be seen above the nose. CBUs are carried underwing.

Below: Underside view of the same F/A-18A as shown in the side view. It is depicted with four Paveway "smart" LGBs (laser-guided bombs), plus a centreline tank and self-defence Sidewinders.

MODERN ATTACK AIRCRAFT

McDonnell Douglas/British Aerospace AV-8B/Harrier II

Origin: Joint prime contractors McDonnell Douglas USA, and British Aerospace, UK.
Engine: One 21,750lb (9,869kg) thrust Rolls-Royce F402-406A Pegasus 105 vectored-thrust turbofan.
Dimensions: Span 30ft 4in (9.25m); length 46ft 4in (14.12m) (TAV, 50ft 3in, 15.32m); height 11ft 8in (3.56m); wing area 230sq ft (21.37m²).
Weights: Empty 12,750lb (5,783kg); max (VTO) 19,185lb (8,702kg), (STO) 31,000lb (14,061kg).
Performance: Max speed (clean, SL) 668mph (1,075km/h); dive Mach limit 0.93; combat radius (STO, seven Mk 82 bombs plus tanks, lo profile, no loiter) 553 miles (889km); ferry range 2,879 miles (4,633km).
Armament: Seven external pylons, for total external load of 7,000lb (3,175kg) for VTO or 17,000lb (7,711kg) for STO, (GR.5) two additional AAM wing pylons; in addition ventral gun pods for (US) one 25mm GAU-12/U gun and 300 rounds or (RAF) two 25mm Aden each with 100 rounds.
History: First flight (YAV-8B rebuild) 9 November 1978, (AV-8B) November 1981; entry into service (AV-8B) 1983, (GR.5) 1987.

Though developed from the original Harrier, the Harrier II is a totally new aircraft showing remarkable improvement in almost every part.

The original Harrier required a lot of attention, especially during accelerating or decelerating transitions, and suffered from poor all-round view and a traditional cockpit, whereas the Harrier II offers a completely new experience.

The wing is the most obvious difference. Apart from giving greater lift, at the expense of extra drag, it houses much more fuel. With eight sine-wave spars and composite construction it is virtually unbreakable, and the curved Lerx (leading-edge root extensions) enhance combat manoeuvrability. (The only real fault of the Harrier II, in British eyes, is that it was planned as a "superior bomb truck" for the US Marine Corps, whereas the RAF were more interested in air-combat agility and speed.)

Under the wing are six stores pylons (eight on the RAF GR.5), four of them plumbed for tanks. The extra pylons on the GR.5 are in line with the outrigger landing gears and carry AIM-9L Sidewinders. The under-fuselage gun pods serve as LIDs (lift-improvement devices) which provide a cushion of high-pressure air under the aircraft. In the AV-8B a 25mm gun is housed in the left pod with its ammunition fed from the right pod; the GR.5 has two gun/ammunition pods.

In the matter of avionics and EW the Harrier II is dramatically updated, the basic kit including INS (Litton ASN-130A or, in the GR.5, a Ferranti set), digital air-data and weapons computers, large field of view HUD, fibre-optic data highways and comprehensive RWR and ECM systems. The primary weapon-delivery system is the Hughes ARBS (angle/rate bombing system), with dual-wavelength TV/laser target acquisition and tracking. Both variants have a bolt-on FR probe pack, added above the left inlet duct, the probe being extended hydraulically when required.

All RAF GR.5s are to be front-line aircraft for RAF Germany. They will have Martin-Baker Mk 12 seats, stronger leading edges, nose and windshield to meet a severe bird-strike requirement, and considerable internal mission equipment including Marconi/Northrop Zeus active ECM. Another non-standard feature is the Ferranti moving-map display. The RAF will convert pilots on the existing T.4s, but the Marines use two-seat TAV-8Bs.

The Marines expect to receive a total of 300 AV-8Bs, not including four FSD (full-scale development) aircraft or 28 TAVs. In late 1988 production switched to the Night Attack AV-8D with new avionics, to be followed in 1990 by the Dash-408 engine of nearly 25,000lb thrust. The Spanish Navy has 12 EAV-8Bs. The RAF will have 94 aircraft, switching from the GR.5 to the GR.7 Nightbird version in 1990 with upgraded avionics but without the uprated engine.

Below: Side elevation of an early production AV-8B, of which about 200 had been delivered as this book was written. The AV-8D has a blister above the nose.

McDonnell Douglas/British Aerospace AV-8B/Harrier II

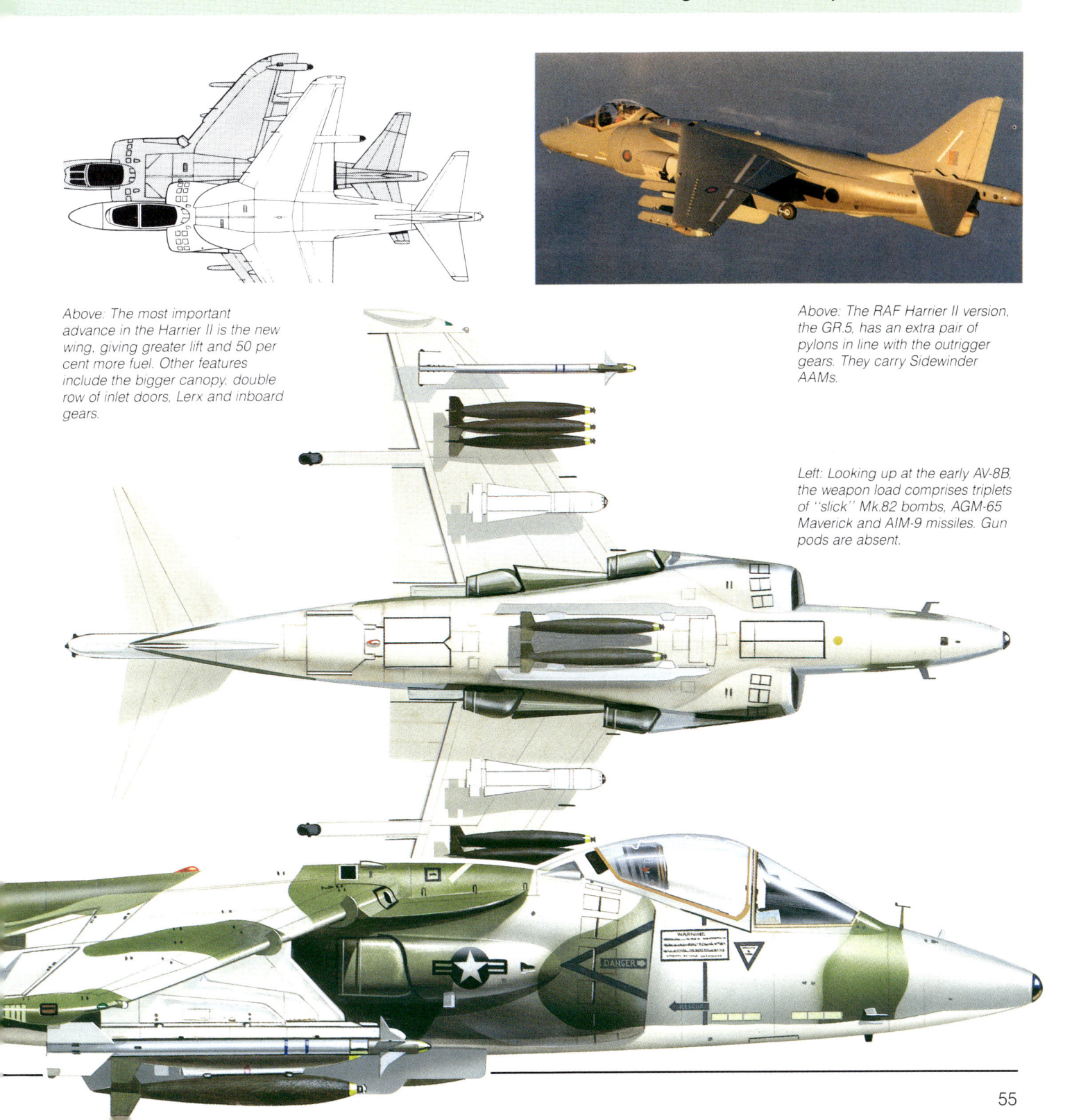

Above: The most important advance in the Harrier II is the new wing, giving greater lift and 50 per cent more fuel. Other features include the bigger canopy, double row of inlet doors, Lerx and inboard gears.

Above: The RAF Harrier II version, the GR.5, has an extra pair of pylons in line with the outrigger gears. They carry Sidewinder AAMs.

Left: Looking up at the early AV-8B, the weapon load comprises triplets of "slick" Mk.82 bombs, AGM-65 Maverick and AIM-9 missiles. Gun pods are absent.

55

MODERN ATTACK AIRCRAFT

MiG-23 and -27 ("Flogger")

Origin: The A. I. Mikoyan design bureau, Soviet Union.
Engine: (most) One 27,560lb (12,500kg) thrust Tumanskii R-29B afterburning turbojet, (27) 25,353lb (11,500kg) Tumanskii R-29-300, (M, UM) 22,485lb (10,200kg) Tumanskii R-27.
Dimensions: Span (72° sweep) 26ft 9.65in (8.17m), (16°) 46ft 9in (14.25m); length (most, excl probe) 55ft 1.4in (16.8m), (BN, 27) 52ft 6in (16.0m); height overall 15ft 10in (4.82m); wing area (16°) 337sq ft (31.3m²).
Weights: Empty (ML) 22,485lb (10,200kg), loaded (clean) (ML) 35,495lb (16,100kg), (27) 34,170lb (15,500kg); max (ML) 41,670lb (18,900kg), (27) 44,312lb (20,100kg).
Performance: Max speed (hi, clean) (23) 1,553mph (2,500km/h, Mach 2.35), (27) 1,124mph (1,800km/h, Mach 1.7); speed at SL (clean) (23) 912mph (1,468km/h, Mach 1.2), (27) 836mph (1,345km/h, Mach 1.1); service ceiling (23) 61,000ft (18,600m), (27) 50,850ft (15,500m); combat radius (23 fighter mission) 560-805 miles (900-1,300km), (27, four FAB-500 and AAMs, lo-lo-lo) 240 miles (390km).
Armament: (MF, ML) One 23mm GSh-23L gun with 200 rounds, two R-23R (AA-7 Apex) and four R-60 (AA-8 Aphid) AAMs; (BN and 27) six-barrel 30mm gun and various bombloads such as 16 FAB-250 or (overload) six FAB-1000 or cluster dispensers, or (glove pylons) two pods with pivoted GSh-23L guns depressed down for attacking surface targets, or two AS-7, -10, -12 or -14 missiles.
History: First flight (Ye-231) probably 1966; entry to service (23S) 1971.

Built at a higher rate than any other combat aircraft throughout 1972-82, the MiG-23 and -27 together constitute the most important single type in the WP air forces, and also were exported in substantial quantities.

The VG wing, which appears to have gone out of fashion in Western nations, gives great lift for takeoff and loiter with heavy loads of fuel and weapons, and in the MiG-23 interceptor roughly doubles the patrol endurance to a maximum of almost 4h. With the wings at 72° supersonic drag is greatly reduced and the aircraft ideally configured for either an air-to-air interception with stand-off kill by missiles or for a lo attack on a surface target.

All versions have more or less the same airframe, designed to a load factor of 8g and for operation from rough airstrips. The first production series was the MiG-23MF, in various sub-types called "Flogger-B" by NATO. This carries J-band radar likened by the USA to that of the F-4J and described as the first Soviet type to have a significant capability against low-level targets; later the 23MF demonstrated an impressive ability to engage targets at far above its own altitude using the large R-23R air-to-air missile.

The trainer has a slimmer nose housing R2L-series radar, two stepped cockpits with separate hinged canopies, a periscope for the instructor at the rear, a sloping sill extending to the front of the windscreen, and a larger dorsal spine fairing. Internal fuel is cut and the engine is the R-27.

The ML, called "Flogger-G", has a smaller dorsal fin and has been seen with a new undernose sensor pod. Later versions have notches at the leading edge of the fixed wing roots, and since 1985 all interceptors have carried the AA-11 Archer missile.

Dedicated attack members of the MiG-23 family are styled MiG-23BN and exist in many variants, some export models having simpler avionics. One, called "Flogger-H", is virtually a MiG-27 with the MiG-23 engine installation, with fully variable inlets and nozzle.

In contrast, the basic MiG-27 is a dedicated subsonic low-level attack aircraft with a simplified propulsion system making no attempt to fly fast at high altitude. It has a new nose with a down-sloping broad profile giving better forward view and accommodating every desired avionic item for the surface attack mission, in place of a radar. Even the cockpit is repositioned at a higher level with a deeper hinged hood and windshield to give the best possible pilot view, plus heavy surrounding armour.

A further change is the fitting of tyres of greater size and reduced inflation pressure for operations from rough unpaved airstrips. The engine has a smaller afterburner with simple nozzle matched to maximum thrust at takeoff and when engaged in low-level missions

Above: This "Flogger-E" trainer was photographed at Tripoli in 1965 (Libyan marking now green).

MiG-23 and -27 ("Flogger")

Below: Looking up at the MiG-23BN, with wings at minimum sweep. There are many subtle differences between versions. The BN retains the fighter's variable inlets for supersonic flight.

Above: Contrasting noses of early Mig-23 fighter versions. From top, the 23ML interceptor; the 23UB tandem dual-control trainer (small radar); the 23MS fighter (small radar).

The oblique forward "chisel" window covers a laser ranger and marked-target seeker. The small radome at the tip of the nose is for air/air ranging in conjunction with the gun. Under the nose is a doppler navigation radar and further aft on each side are small blisters over radar warning receiver antennas. Forward-pointing pods on the fixed wing glove leading edges are ASM guidance transmitters.

The MiG-27 is designed to carry all available tactical missiles, fuel/air explosives, cluster munitions and laser-guided "smart" weapons. From 1980 the main production version had a kinked taileron trailing edge, leading-edge root extension strakes, a complete revision of the nose sensors and no bullet avionics fairings on the wing gloves.

The mixed model equips Nos 10, 220 and 221 Sqns of the Indian Air Force, but the version licence-built by HAL is the MiG-27M "Flogger-J", a pure attack variant with wingroot strakes.

Right: Noses of the MiG-23BN attack aircraft (top) and 23MF interceptor (lower).

Below: Side elevation of a recent MiG-23BN attack aircraft, with "ducknose" but variable inlets.

MODERN ATTACK AIRCRAFT

Mitsubishi F-1 and T-2

Origin: Mitsubishi Heavy Industries Ltd., Japan.
Engines: Two Ishikawajima-Harima TF40-801A (licence-built Rolls-Royce/Turbomeca Adour 102) augmented turbofans with max rating of 7,305lb (3,314kg).
Dimensions: Span 25ft 10in (7.87m); length 58ft 7in (17.86m); height 14ft 5in (4.39m); wing area 227.9sq ft (21.17m²).
Weights: Empty (T-2) 13,905lb (6,307kg); (F-1) 14,017lb (6,358kg); loaded (T-2, clean) 21,274lb (9,650kg); (T-2 max) 28,440lb (12,900kg); (F-1 max) 30,203lb (13,701kg).
Performance: Max speed (at clean gross weight) 1,056mph (1,700km/h, Mach 1.6); initial climb 35,000ft (10,670m)/min; service ceiling 50,025ft (15,250m); range (T-2 with external tanks) 1,610 miles (2,593km); (F-1 with eight 500lb bombs) 700 miles (1,126km).
Armament: (T-2A, F-1) One 20mm JM61 multi-barrel gun under left side of cockpit floor, with ammunition drum containing 750 rounds; pylon hardpoints under centreline and inboard and outboard on wings, with light stores attachments at tips. Total weapon load (T-2A) normally 2,000lb (907kg); (F-1) 6,000lb (2,722kg) comprising 12×500lb bombs, eight 500lb plus two tanks of 183gal, or two 1,300lb (590kg) ASM-1 anti-ship missiles, and four Sidewinders.
History: First flight (XT-2) 20 July 1971; (T-2A) January 1975; (FST-2) June 1975; service delivery (T-2A) March 1975; (F-1) 1977.

The T-2 was strongly influenced by the Anglo-French Jaguar, and has the same configuration and engines. Unusual in being a supersonic trainer, it has a simple Mitsubishi Electric search/ranging radar and a Thomson-CSF HUD. The JASDF bought a total of 28 T-2 trainers, plus 58 of the armed T-2A combat trainer version. All were delivered by 1984; one being grossly modified to serve as a CCV research aircraft.

The F-1, originally known as the FST-2, has the same airframe, engines and systems, but is a single seater, the rear cockpit being occupied by avionics. A Ferranti inertial nav/attack system is fitted, together with a different Mitsubishi AWG-12 radar with air/air and air/ground modes, a weapon-aiming computer, radar altimeter and RHAWS, the weapon system being modified from 1982 to handle the locally developed ASM-1 anti-ship missile, which has active radar guidance and a maximum range of 31 miles (50km).

Though the ASM-1 remains the principal weapon carried, the F-1 can also carry four JLAU-3A launchers each with 19 rockets of 70mm calibre, or four RL-7 with seven 70mm or four RL-4 with four of 125mm size. Other weapons now being introduced are bombs of 500 or 750lb fitted with US-derived smart laser guidance. Research has been in hand for several years on a longer-ranged successor missile to the ASM-1.

Between 1980 and 1987 Mitsubishi delivered a total of 77 F-1 aircraft to the JASDF. They serve with the 3rd Wing at Misawa and the 8th Wing at Tsuiki. All surviving aircraft are to undergo a life-extension programme to keep them operational until 1995.

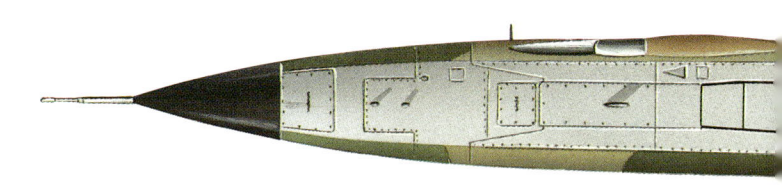

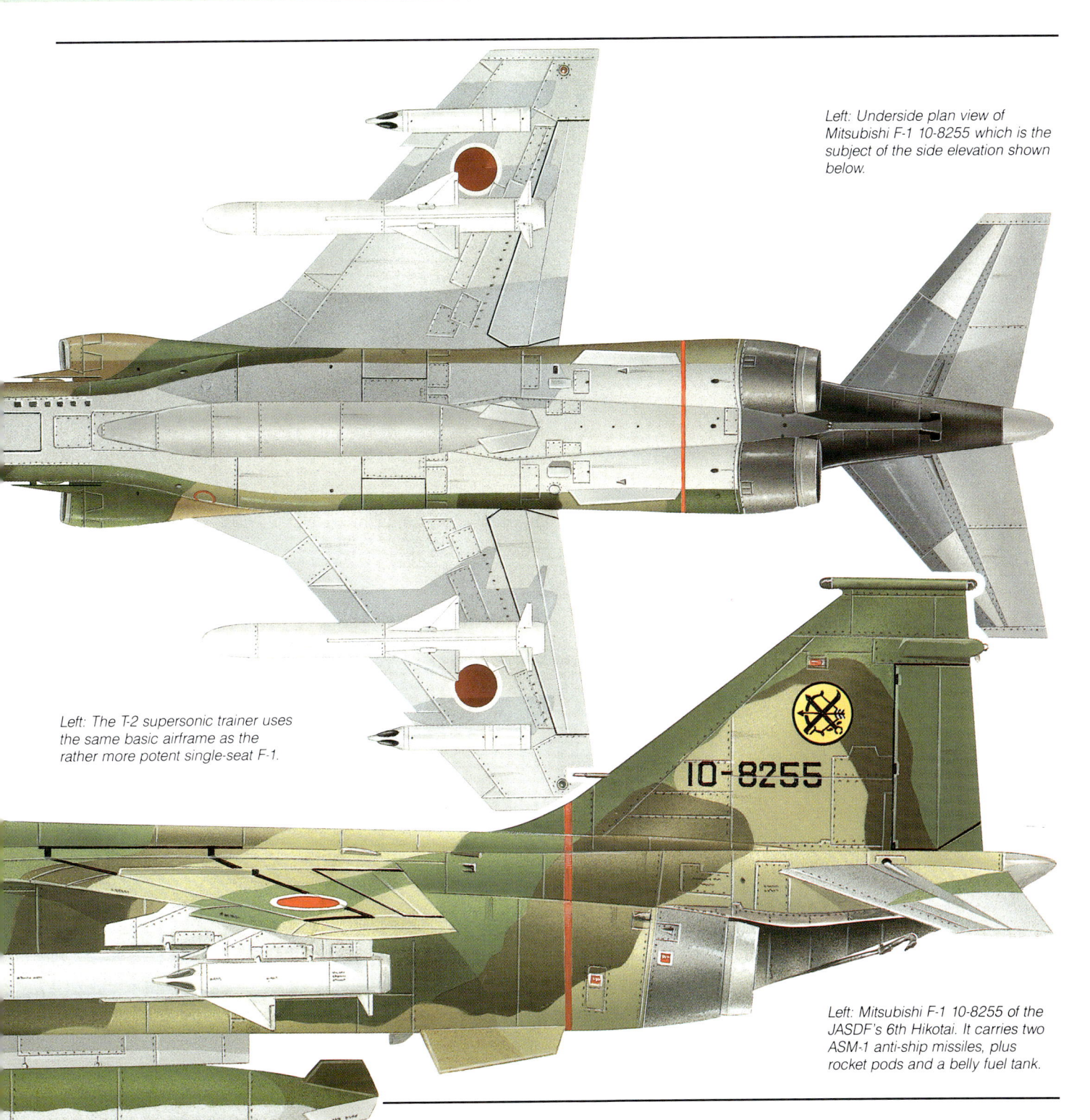

Mitsubishi F-1 and T-2

Left: Underside plan view of Mitsubishi F-1 10-8255 which is the subject of the side elevation shown below.

Left: The T-2 supersonic trainer uses the same basic airframe as the rather more potent single-seat F-1.

Left: Mitsubishi F-1 10-8255 of the JASDF's 6th Hikotai. It carries two ASM-1 anti-ship missiles, plus rocket pods and a belly fuel tank.

59

MODERN ATTACK AIRCRAFT

NAMC Q-5 (A-5)

Origin: Chinese State factory at Nanchang.
Engines: Two 7,167lb (3,250kg) thrust Wopen-6 afterburning turbojets (Tumanskii R-9BF-811); (Q-5A) 8,267lb (3,750kg) WP-6A.
Dimensions: Span 31ft 10in (9.7m); length (inc probe) 53ft 4in (16.255m); height overall 14ft 9.56in (4.51m); wing area 300.85 sq ft (27.95m²).
Weights: Empty 14,317lb (6,494kg); loaded (clean) 21,010lb (9,530kg); (max) 26,455lb (12,000kg).
Performance: Max speed (hi, clean) 740mph (1,190km/h, Mach 1.12); (SL, clean) 752mph (1,210km/h, Mach 0.99); service ceiling 52,500ft (16,000m); TO run (max wt) 4,100ft (1,250m); combat radius (max bombs, no afterburner) (hi-lo-hi) 248 miles (400km).
Armament: Two 23mm single-barrel guns, each with 100 rounds, in wing roots; internal bomb bay usually occupied by fuel tank, leaving four fuselage pylons each rated at 551lb (250kg) and four wing pylons, those inboard of landing gear being rated at 551lb (250kg) and those outboard being plumbed for 167gal (760lit) drop tanks. Max bomb or other stores load usually 4,410lb (2,000kg).
History: First flight 1972; service delivery believed 1976.

Below: One of the original Nanchang A5 production aircraft. Versions which have appeared subsequently feature completely revised avionics suites and more powerful Wopen WP-6A turbojet engines.

Panavia Tornado IDS

Origin: Panavia Aircraft GmbH, formed by British Aerospace, MBB of W. Germany and Aeritalia.
Engines: Two Turbo-Union RB199 Mk 103 augmented turbofans each rated at 16,920lb (7,675kg) thrust with full afterburner.
Dimensions: Span (25°) 45ft 7.24in (13.90m), (67°) 28ft 2.6in (8.60m); length 54ft 10in (16.7m); height 19ft 6in (5.95m); wing area not published.
Weights: Empty (equipped) 31,065lb (14,091kg); loaded (clean) about 45,000lb (20,411kg); max loaded, about 60,000lb (28,150kg).
Performance: Max speed (clean), at sea level, over 920mph (1,480km/h, Mach 1.2), at height, over 1,452mph (2,337km/h, Mach 2.2); service ceiling over 50,000ft (15,240m); combat radius (8,000lb/3,629kg bombs, hi-lo-hi) 863 miles (1,390km).
Armament: Two 27mm Mauser cannon each with 180 rounds; seven pylons, three tandem on body and four on the swinging wings, for external load up to 19,840lb (9,000kg).
History: First flight (prototype) 14 August 1974, service delivery (IDS to trials unit) February 1978, (squadron service) 1982.

Though from the start a multirole aircraft, the Tornado IDS (interdiction strike) is optimized to the long-range all-weather blind first-pass attack mission against the most heavily defended surface targets, including ships. It is the most capable aircraft of its size ever built.

On typical missions its fuel burn is roughly equal to that of an F-16, 60 per cent that of an F-4 and about 50 per cent that of an F-15 or Su-24, while carrying at least as heavy and

Right: This aircraft, from production batch 2, was completed as a British GR.1 and became 05 of 27 Sqn in 1983. Later, it went to 617 "Dam Busters" Squadron.

NAMC Q-5 (A-5)

The first really major military aircraft to be designed in the People's Republic, the Q-5 was based on the J-6 but differs in almost every part. The chief change was to extend the forward fuselage, terminate the air inlet ducts in lateral inlets and add an internal weapons bay. The wings were extended at the roots, which also increased the track of the landing gear (which is strengthened to handle the much greater weights), and the vertical tail was made taller. The cockpit was redesigned, and enclosed by an upward-hinged canopy leading into a different fuselage spine. There were many systems changes, most important being an increase in internal fuel capacity of nearly 70 per cent.

Performance proved adequate with the original engines, though at high weights a good runway is needed, and a braking parachute is normally streamed (later aircraft have it housed in a pod below the rudder as in later J-6s).

At first it was thought the reason for using lateral inlets was to enable a radar to be installed, but this was mistaken. Q-5 development aircraft have flown with radar, and a small gunsight ranging set is fitted to some recent aircraft, but it was not until 1986 that development started on the Q-5M described later. Avionics are described as fully adequate for visual attack missions.

The Pakistan AF, first customer for the A-5 export version, was delighted with the batch of 52 delivered from 1983 and equipping Nos. 16, 26 and 7 Sqns. Eventually, it expects to receive 140 A-5s, to arm eight squadrons and an OCU.

The photographs so far seen of the A-5 show it to be cleaner than regular Q-5s, though the avionic standards are said to be similar. Chinese Q-5s can carry nuclear bombs of from 5 to 20kT yield, and the usual method of delivery of these is a toss. Conventional weapons are usually aimed by the SH-IJ optical sight in a dive attack.

In 1986 the Chinese industry signed an agreement with Aeritalia for a 30-month development programme to upgrade the Q-5 to Q-5M standard. This incorporates the nav/attack avionics of the AMX and also is powered by the WP-6A (Wopen-6A) with the rating given in the specification. The new digital avionics make the Q-5M a formidable aircraft which is offered for export as the A-5M. Flight testing of two prototypes was to be completed in late 1988, with deliveries beginning in 1989.

Panavia Tornado IDS

varied a load of weapons as the best of these aircraft over a considerably greater unrefuelled range.

Features include a Texas Instruments multimode radar with programmable software, a TFR (terrain-following radar), electrically signalled FBW (fly-by-wire) flight controls with artificial stability, fully variable supersonic inlets (which help make this the fastest aircraft in the world at low level), advanced avionic systems to manage the array of stores which can be carried and modern tandem cockpits with head-up and head-down displays in the front and three electronic displays in the back.

Among the stores which have been cleared are all tactical

Above: Three aircraft from No.4 batch, serving with Italy's 36th Stormo at Gioia del Colle, near Bari in southern Italy.

MODERN ATTACK AIRCRAFT

bombs of the four initial customers, nine rocket pods, Sidewinder AAMs and Sea Eagle, Kormoran, Maverick, Alarm, GBU-15, Paveway, AS.30 and AS.30L, Martel (seldom to be carried), Aspide, BL.755, JP.233 and MW-1; Harpoon and possibly other cruise missiles may be carried later.

All aircraft have two guns, Martin-Baker Mk 10 automatic zero/zero seats, a gas-turbine APU, automatically scheduled lift-dumpers, pre-armed engine reversers, anti-skid brakes and (as a further option) a braking parachute. There is provision to bolt on an FR probe on the right side below the canopy. All sub-types have comprehensive EW systems, with advanced RHAWS and either the Elettronica EL/73 deception jammer and ELT 553 ECM pod, AEG Cerberus, or Marconi Avionics Sky Shadow.

RAF squadrons began with Nos. 9, 27 and 617, followed by eight in RAF Germany: 15, 16 and 20 at Laarbruch, 14, 17 and 31 of the former Jaguar wing at Brüggen, No. 9 at Brüggen (from Honington) and, in 1988, No. 2 (II) Sqn at Laarbruch with reconnaissance-dedicated aircraft.

Marineflieger MFG 1 and 2 are both converted from the F-104G, while the Luftwaffe equipped four JaboG wings, Nos. 31 to 34. Italy's AMI is using 54 aircraft to replace the F/RF-104G in the 6° Stormo's 154° and 155° Gruppi plus the 36° Stormo's 156° Gruppi.

Total national commitments, all delivered or in process of manufacture as this was written, comprise: RAF 228 with designation GR.1 (plus a pre-production machine brought up to GR.1 standard); Marineflieger, 112; Luftwaffe, 212; and AMI 99 plus one pre-production aircraft updated. All these will be put through differing mid-life update programmes to fit them for service beyond 2010. Further IDS aircraft have been ordered by Saudi Arabia (48), Jordan (8) and Malaysia (12) and more are expected to be in the eighth batch, together with an ECR (electronic combat and reconnaissance) version for the Luftwaffe and Italy. (The ADV interceptor is described in the companion book on fighters.)

Left: Looking up at ZA542, an RAF Tornado GR.1 featured on the previous page. It is depicted with a typical load of body-hung bombs, tanks, BOZ chaff pod and Sky Shadow jammer pod.

This page, far right: One of the first Tornados became the Luftwaffe's 43-20, serving at the Trinational Tornado Training Establishment at RAF Cottesmore.

Panavia Tornado IDS

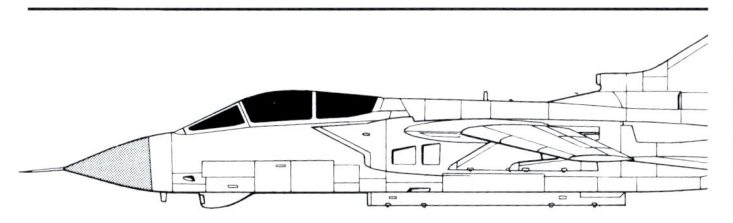

Above: Features of the IDS version discussed in this book include TI main radar, and (RAF only) an undernose laser.

Below: For comparison, this shows the longer nose of the ADV interceptor version (also see plan view below right).

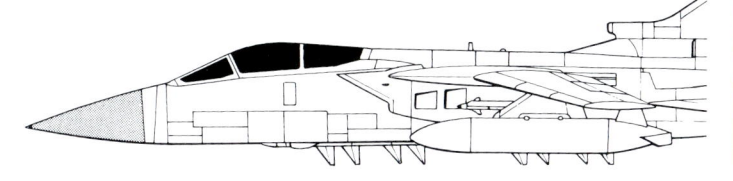

Above: An early prototype Tornado, carrying various dummy stores, engaged in testing TFR (terrain-following radar) among mountains.

Left: Looking down on ZA542 (see opposite and previous pages) with the wings at maximum sweep and BOZ on right outer pylon.

Right: This underside view shows how four Sky Flash missiles are carried under the fuselage of the ADV interceptor. This forced the fuselage to be lengthened, giving Panavia an option of a stretched attack model.

63

MODERN ATTACK AIRCRAFT

Saab 37 Viggen

Origin: Saab-Scania AB, Sweden.
Engine: One 25,970lb (11,790kg) Svenska Flygmotor RM8A (licence-built Pratt & Whitney JT8D turbofan redesigned in Sweden for Mach 2 with afterburner).
Dimensions: Span of main wing 34ft 9.3in (10.6m); length (AJ) 53ft 5.7in (16.3m); height 18ft 4.5in (5.6m), wing area 495.1sq ft (46.0m²).
Weights: Empty (all) about 27,000lb (12,250kg); loaded, (AJ normal armament) 35,275lb (16,000kg), (AJ max weapons) 45,195lb (20,500kg).
Performance: Max speed (clean) about 1,320mph (2,135km/h, Mach 2), or Mach 1.1 at sea level; initial climb, about 40,000ft (12,200m)/min (time from start of take-off run to 32,800/10,000m = 100sec); service ceiling, 60,000ft (18,300m); tactical radius with external stores (not drop tanks), hi-lo-hi profile, over 620 miles (1,000km).
Armament: Seven pylons (option: nine) for aggregate external load of 13,200lb (6,000kg), including RB04, 05 or 75 missiles for attack, and RB24 and 28 missiles for defence.
History: First flight 8 February 1967; (production AJ) 23 February 1971; service delivery (AJ) June 1971.

Like all Swedish programmes for combat aircraft the Type 37 Viggen (Thunderbolt) has been wholly successful, producing five sub-types of the same basic machine, each tailored to a different primary role, within budget and on time. The first and most numerous version is the AJ37, dedicated mainly to attack surface targets and ships.

From the start the design was biased in favour of STOL operations from rough strips, including straight stretches of country highways and dirt tracks. The big afterburning engine gives high thrust for quick getaway, though at the cost of temporary high fuel consumption. The large delta wing and canard foreplane form a powerful high-lift combination, and can pull tight turns down to low airspeeds. On landing the Viggen can be brought in at only 137mph (220km/h), slammed on to the ground in a carrier-type no-flare impact, and given reverse thrust and maximum no-skid wheel braking.

The AJ37 carries the RB04E cruise missile which homes on ships and packs a tremendous punch, the RB05A which can be used against ground, naval and certain airborne targets, and the RB75 Maverick TV-guided precision ASM. For air-to-air use gun pods, usually of 30mm Aden type, can be carried, as well as the RB24 Sidewinder and RB28 Falcon AAMs.

The AJ37 equips two squadrons of F6 wing at Karlsborg, two squadrons of F7 at Satenäs and one squadron of F15 at Söderhamm. Variants of the AJ37 are the SF37 and SH37 reconnaissance models.

The SH37, for maritime use, replaced the S32C Lansen in F13 Wing and in mixed SH/SF Wings F17 and F21. It is used primarily to survey, register and report all maritime activity near Sweden. It has the basic airframe of the AJ37, with an LM Ericsson multimode radar, Marconi HUD and central digital computer, with an added camera for recording the radar displays. The three fuselage pylons carry a large tank on the centreline, a night reconnaissance pod with IR linescan and LLTV on the left and a Red Baron or long-range camera pod on the right. Inboard wing pylons can carry active or passive ECM jammer pods, and very complete Elint and EW recorders are carried, together with a tape recorder and a data camera which records film co-ordination figures, date, time, aircraft position, course, height, target location and other information.

The SF37 has no nose radar, and its slim, pointed nose houses four vertical or oblique cameras for low-level use, two long-range vertical high-altitude cameras and VKA IR linescan. Also installed in the fuselage are the camera sight, an IR sensor and EW systems including an RWR and Elint recorders. The sensors give 180° horizon-to-horizon coverage and are specially arranged to work on wavelengths which reveal the presence of camouflaged targets. External loads can include the centreline tanks and active or passive electronic counter-measures pods on the inboard wing pylons.

The JA37 interceptor is featured in the companion work on modern fighters.

64

Saab 37 Viggen

Above: Like the JA37 fighter the Sk37 trainer has a tall fin with a sweptback tip.

Above: This is the standard vertical tail as fitted to the AJ37, SF37 and SH37.

Left: Head-on views showing (1) the folding vertical tail for use of underground hangars, (2) the AJ37 body pylons, (3) the ventral gun pack of the JA37 fighter and (4) an SH37 sensor pod.

Above: The attack AJ37 flies with several Flygvapen units including F15 Wing.

Right: Underside view of an AJ37 showing armament of two RB05s and four rocket pods.

Above: Side elevation of an AJ37 in service with F7 Wing at Satenäs.

65

MODERN ATTACK AIRCRAFT

SEPECAT Jaguar

Origin: SEPECAT, consortium formed by British Aerospace and Dassault-Breguet, France.
Engines: Two Rolls-Royce/Turbomeca Adour augmented turbofans: (A, E) 7,305lb (3,313kg) Adour 102; (GR. 1, T.2) 8,040lb (3,647kg) Adour 104; (International) 8,400lb (3,810kg) Adour 811.
Dimensions: Span 28ft 6in (8.69m): length (except T.2, E) 55ft 3in (16.83m); (T.2, E) 57ft 6in (17.53m); height 16ft 0.5in (4.89m); wing area 260.27sq ft (24.18m²).
Weights: Empty, about 15,432lb (7,000kg); "normal takeoff" (internal fuel and gun ammunition) 24,149lb (10,954kg); max 34,612lb (15,700kg).
Performance: Max speed (lo, some external stores) 840mph (1,350km/h, Mach 1.1), (hi, some external stores) 1,055mph (1,700km/h, Mach 1.6); attack radius, no external fuel, hi-lo-hi with bombs, 530 miles (852km); ferry range 2,614 miles (4,210km).
Armament: (A, E) Two 30mm DEFA 553 each with 150 rounds; five pylons for total external load of 10,500lb (4,763kg); GR.1 as above but guns two 30mm Aden; (T.2) as above but single Aden; (International) various, guns Aden or DEFA, often overwing AIM-9P or Magic AAMs and various ASMs.
History: First flight (E) 8 September 1968; (production E) 2 November 1971; (GR.1) 11 October 1972.

Originally developed jointly in an Anglo-French project for a light attack aircraft and supersonic trainer, the Jaguar actually matured as one of the most effective attack aircraft of its day.

Features of the basic aircraft include a small but efficient high-mounted wing, with full-span double-slotted flaps, spoilers for roll control (supplemented by the tailerons) and powered slats which can be used in combat. The extremely small engines are fed by plain inlets, and instead of going for Mach 2 the designers aimed at good agility, comprehensive avionics, and the ability to operate from rough unsurfaced strips with heavy weapon loads. The main landing gears have long-stroke levered suspension, low-pressure twin tyres on each leg, and anti-skid brakes, the latter being backed up by a braking chute and arrester hook. The cockpit has an upward hinged canopy (two in the tandem dual version) and a Martin-Baker Mk 9 zero-zero seat (French Jaguars have the earlier Mk 4 seat). The two-seater has the same internal fuel capacity as other versions, the extra cockpit being added in the nose at the expense of some avionics and one gun.

The RAF Jaguar GR.1 has a full INS (recently updated together with a revised cockpit), HUD, projected-map display and laser in a "chisel nose", as well as engines uprated as a field modification. A total of 203 was delivered. A standard fitment has been the ARI.18223 passive RWR system, but there has been little ECM protection other than extremely low flying. In 1983 an interim fit of six jammer/chaff cartridges

Below: Taken a few years ago, before the unit converted to Tornado, two No. 20 Squadron Jaguars carry practice bomb dispensers beneath the fuselage.

Below: Side elevation of a Jaguar GR.1 of RAF No. 226 OCU, the conversion unit at Lossiemouth, Morayshire.

SEPECAT Jaguar

was added in a box under the parachute bay, and BAe has been fitting a new RWR, jammer pod and Phimat chaff dispenser.

The Armée de l'Air Jaguar A has a simpler avionic system, with twin-gyro platform and doppler, but the final 30 of the 200 of both A and E (two-seat) Jaguars are equipped with the Atlis II TV/laser pod used in conjunction with Matra smart bombs and the AS.30L laser-homing ASM. French Jaguars equip ECs (Escadres de Chasse) at St Dizier and Toul-Rosières, with subordinate elements at Istres and Bordeaux respectively.

There were numerous customer options in the export Jaguar International, most of which have uprated engines and avionics based on those of the GR.1. Ecuador bought 12, and the 24 for Oman have a Marconi Avionics 920C computer and carry Sidewinder AAMs. The most advanced Jaguars so far exported are those of India, where 40 were delivered from BAe, 45 more were assembled by HAL and 31 more are of HAL manufacture. Those tasked in the attack role have an RAF-type HUD or (on HAL-assembled aircraft) a new HUD and weapon-aiming system similar to that of the Sea Harrier 5, with the Magic AAM used for self-defence. Anti-ship Jaguars have the Agave nose radar (with optional chin laser) and AM 39 Exocet missiles.

The final order for new-build Jaguars was for 18 for Nigeria. One RAF GR.1 is serving as a research aircraft in a totally unstable CCV configuration. Total production was 497 in Europe plus 31 in India.

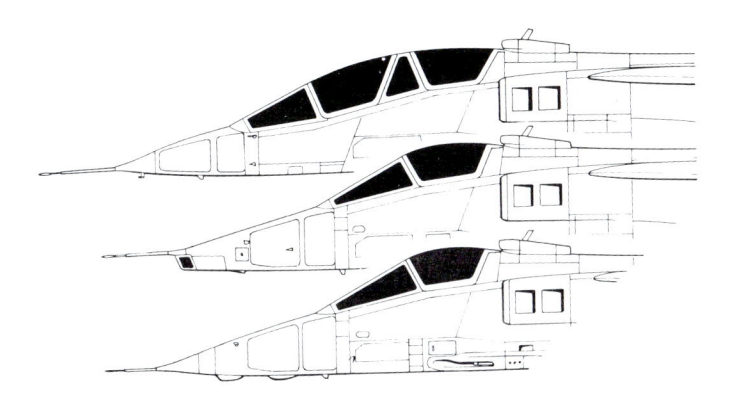

Above: Noses of contrasting versions. From the top, they are the tandem-seat trainer; the GR.1 and International with the "chisel nose" and the French Jaguar A. These drawings also show various standard features such as the air-conditioning duct behind the cockpit and the two square auxiliary air inlets.

Right: Looking up at the same GR.1 we see four BL.755 cluster bomb dispensers, two AIM-9s and two tanks.

67

MODERN ATTACK AIRCRAFT

Sukhoi Su-17/-20/-22 ("Fitter")

Origin: The design bureau named for P. O. Sukhoi, Soviet Union.
Engines: (early) One Lyul'ka AL-21F-3 afterburning turbojet with ratings of 17,200/24,700lb (7,800/11,200kg); (current variants) one Tumanskii R-29BS-300 afterburning turbojet with ratings of 17,635/25,352lb (8,000/11,500kg).
Dimensions: Span (28°) 45ft 3in (13.8m), (62°) 32ft 10in (10.0m); length (basic-17 incl nose probes) 61ft 6.2in (18.75m), (later variants) 62ft 9in (19.13m); wing area (28°) 431.6sq ft (40.1m²).
Weights: (estimated) Empty (Fitter-C) 22,050lb (10,000kg), (-H) 22,500lb (10,200kg), loaded (clean) (-C) 30,865lb (14,000kg), (-H) 34,170lb (15,500kg); max loaded (-C) 39,020lb (17,700kg), (-H) 42,330lb (19,200kg).
Performance: Max speed (clean, typical), (SL) 800mph (1,290km/h, Mach 1.05), (36,000ft/11,000m), 1,380mph (2,220km/h, Mach 2.09), (SL, with typical external stores) 650mph (1,050km/h); initial climb (clean) 45,275ft (13,800m)/min; service ceiling 59,050ft (18,000m); combat radius (-C, 2t bombload, hi-lo-hi) 391 miles (630km), (-H, 3t bombload, hi-lo-hi) 435 miles (700km).
Armament: Two NR-30 guns each with 70 rounds and two K-13A (Atoll) or R-60 (Aphid) AAM; eight pylons for load exceeding 7,000lb (3,175kg) including tanks, ASMs, reconnaissance pods or ECM jammers.
History: First flight (Su-22IG) 1966; (production -17) probably 1970.

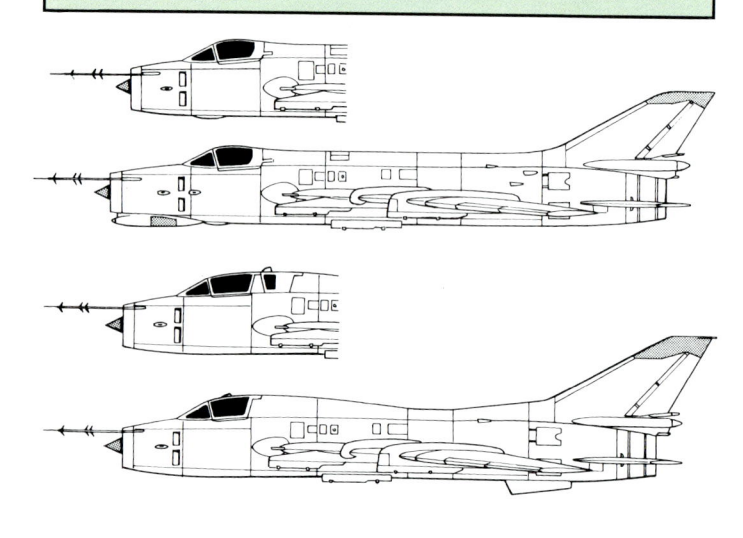

The Su-22IG (IG meaning variable geometry in Russian) was an Su-7 with just the outer portions of its wings pivoted. From 1972 until 1987 many successively improved examples were put into use by Soviet Frontal Aviation, AVMF (Naval Aviation) and WP air forces. Others have been exported.

The perfection of this partial "swing-wing" configuration came in 1963. Sukhoi had already planned improvements to the Su-7 involving later engines, dorsal spines of increasing size (as seen on the MiG-21), greater weapon loads and improved EW suites. The first stage was adoption of the big AL-21 engine which, despite its smoke at full power, burns less fuel than the AL-7 while giving greater thrust.

In round figures the Su-17 lifts twice the weapon load over mission radii increased by 30 per cent while eliminating ATO rockets and yet using airstrips half as long as previously! At the same time control input forces are reduced and inflight agility is improved, both turn radii and rate of roll being better.

Many of these early Su-17s are still in use, along with improved models with a longer nose housing a laser ranger in the conical inlet centrebody and a chin fairing which among other things accommodates a doppler navigation radar. Almost all aircraft, including two-seaters (which have a down-tilted forward fuselage to improve view), have eight stores pylons. Some, including two-seaters, have only one gun, on the right.

The non-fighter designations Su-20 and -22 were applied to all subsequent variants, the former being the export Su-17

Above: Comparative features of, from the top: the initial production Su-17 (very like the fixed-wing Su-7BM); the S-32M version, with longer nose and undernose sensors; the U-32 (Su-17UM) trainer; and the Su-22 with the Tumanskii engine and other changes.

Sukhoi Su-17/-20/-22 ("Fitter")

(including aircraft for WP countries), which all have various avionic deletions compared with those in Soviet service. Peru complained that its first batches were gravely lacking in navaids, had an almost useless Sirena 2 RWR and were fitted with IFF (not the usual SRO-2M) which was incompatible with SA-3 "Goa" SAMs supplied at almost the same time!

By this time Peru had signed for later variants, called "Fitter-F" and "Fitter-J" by NATO, the latter being a member of the final sub-family with the later-technology Tumanskii engine. Features of these aircraft include a deeper spine providing a major increase in internal fuel, a raised and redesigned cockpit giving a better pilot view and more room for additional avionics, two extra pylons, slightly bulging rear fuselage, and a vertical tail of increased height, with a dorsal fin, and added ventral fin.

Two-seaters of this family have a cockpit and canopy arrangement totally different from earlier versions, with a small metal rear canopy with a square window on each side.

Later variants have zero/zero seats, while earlier aircraft have rocket-assisted seats for zero height above 87mph (140km/h). A further addition is air-conditioning, and the final model has a ram inlet at the front of the dorsal fin.

Above: Soviet Frontal Aviation has about 1,000 Su-17s, the latest being "Fitter-H/K".

Below: Looking up at the Peruvian S-32M (Su-17M), with outer wings at minimum sweep. This shows the maximum load of eight GP bombs.

Below: Side elevation of an S-32M (Soviet air forces Su-17M). The longer nose houses a laser ranger and marked-target seeker and a doppler navigation radar.

69

MODERN ATTACK AIRCRAFT

Sukhoi Su-24 ("Fencer")

Origin: The design bureau named for P. O. Sukhoi, Soviet Union.
Engines: Two afterburning engines (see below).
Dimensions: (estimated) Span (16°) 57ft 5in (17.5m); (68°) 34ft 5.5in (10.5m); length overall 69ft 10in (21.29m); height 19ft 8in (6.0m); wing area (16°) 500sq ft (46.4m²).
Weights: (estimated) Empty 41,885lb (19,000kg); loaded (clean) 64,000lb (29,000kg); max 90,390lb (41,000kg).
Performance: Max speed (clean, 36,000ft/11,000m) 1,440mph (2,315km/h, Mach 2.18), (max external load, SL) about 620mph (1,000km/h); service ceiling (with weapons) 57,400ft (17,500m); combat radius (lo-lo-lo, 8t bombload) 200 miles (322km), (lo-lo-hi, 2.5t bombload) 590 miles (950km), (hi-lo-hi, 2,500kg bombload) 1,115 miles (1,800km).
Armament: Eight identical MERs (multiple ejector racks) for total load of 24,250lb (11,000kg); glove pylons plumbed for largest drop tanks seen on Soviet aircraft; one gun (see below).
History: First flight believed 1969; service entry 1974.

Spurred by the USAF TFX (F-111) programme, this aircraft was planned at the same time. Despite its age the consensus of Western opinion is that the Su-24 is powered by the AL-21F-3, or a close relative. Thrust with max augmentation is in the 25,000lb (11,340kg) class.

The Su-24 resembles the Tornado, though on a larger scale; it follows the F-111 in side-by-side seating for the pilot and weapon-systems officer. Unlike the F-111 it has half its heavy weapon load under the fuselage. Max wing loading is some 180lb/sq ft (878kg/m²), and combined with the max sweep of 68deg and near-absence of a fixed portion must result in outstandingly good ride qualities in low-level missions at full power.

Other airframe features include fully variable engine inlets, with auxiliary doors and ejectors; slender wings with full-span slats and double-slotted flaps; roll control by wing spoilers (at low speeds) and powered tailerons; a single vertical tail plus ventral fins at the chines of the wide flat-bottomed rear fuselage; and the best overall avionic fit seen on any tactical aircraft in service anywhere.

The main radar is a pulse-doppler set of remarkable power and versatility. Terrain-following capability is provided by

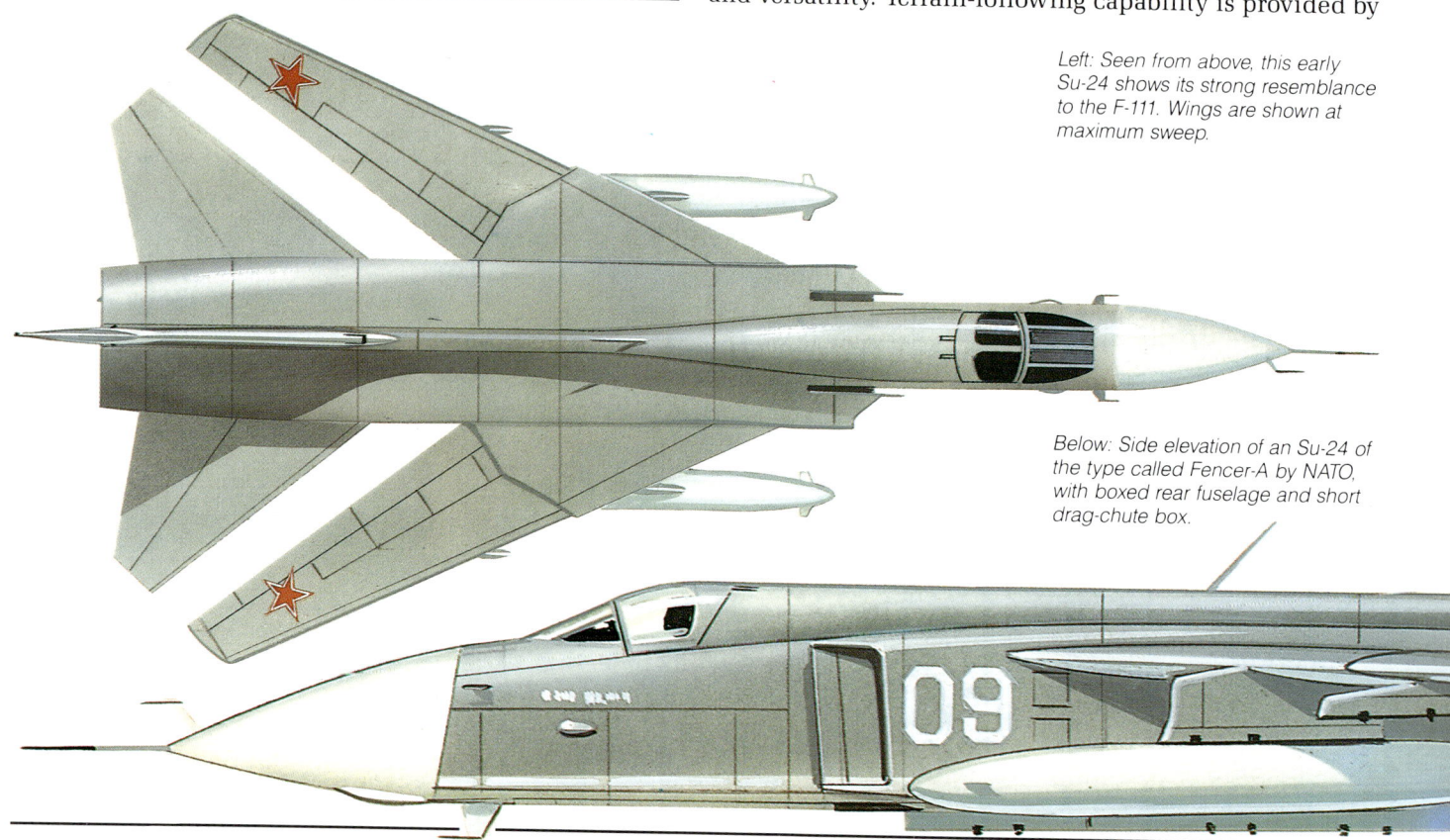

Left: Seen from above, this early Su-24 shows its strong resemblance to the F-111. Wings are shown at maximum sweep.

Below: Side elevation of an Su-24 of the type called Fencer-A by NATO, with boxed rear fuselage and short drag-chute box.

Sukhoi Su-24 ("Fencer")

secondary TFR sets and a separate doppler navigation radar is on the ventral centreline. The entire aircraft is covered with avionics, most of them flush or served by small blisters. A laser ranger and marked-target seeker is in a small chin fairing, what are believed to be ECM jammers are ahead of the wing gloves on the top sides of the inlets, and the tail is a forest of flush aerials and small pods or blisters, varying from one aircraft to another.

NATO analysts have found difficulty in identifying the two ventral blisters, which cover permanently installed equipment. In the author's opinion both are guns, but of different types, in conformity with Soviet policy for use against different classes of target, but the official view is that only the left installation is a gun, the right-hand one being unidentified.

At the time of writing the number of Su-24s in service was put at 900. They are serving in all peripheral Military Districts of the Soviet Union, the main concentration being in Europe but over 200 being around China and on the Pacific coastal areas. The two giant Su-24 forces are the 4th Air Army (Hungary and the Ukraine) and the 24th Air Army (Poland), each of which has five Su-24 polks (regiments) with 60 inventory aircraft apiece. According to the US Defense Department, some Su-24s are now being assigned to the ADD (long-range aviation) strategic force, "and the number assigned to this task is likely to increase by 50 per cent over the next few years".

So far five production versions have been identified, known in the West only by the code names allocated by the NATO alliance.

Fencer-A is the original model, with a rectangular rear fuselage box around the jetpipes. Fencer-B and subsequent versions have the rear fuselage curved tightly round the nozzles, and a larger brake-chute compartment just above. Fencer-C (1981) introduced the avionics fairings ahead of the wing roots, and on the sides of the fin cap, as well as a multi-prong nose probe. Fencer-D (1983) has a flight refuelling probe, slightly extended dorsal fin, longer nose, ventral blister (thought to be a FLIR) and giant fences built into the wing glove pylons. Fencer-E is an AVMF Baltic Fleet version replacing the Tu-16 in reconnaissance and attack missions. Fencer-F is expected to be the designation of a dedicated electronic warfare version which is due to replace Yak-28s, and which was on test in 1988.

Right: Photographs of later versions of Su-24 showing (upper photo) a Fencer-D in landing configuration, and (lower photo) a Fencer-D which was intercepted by Swedish fighters over the Baltic.

MODERN ATTACK AIRCRAFT

Sukhoi Su-25 ("Frogfoot")

Origin: The design bureau named for P. O. Sukhoi, Soviet Union.
Engines: Two 9,340lb (4,237kg) Tumanskii R-13-300 turbojets.
Dimensions: Span 46ft 11in (14.3m); length 50ft 6.3in (15.4m); height 15ft 9in (4.8m); wing area 362.7sq ft (33.7m)².
Weights: Empty 20,950lb (9,500kg); max (depending on airstrip strength) 39,950-42,330lb (18,120-19,200kg).
Performance: Max speed (low level, clean) 608mph (980km/h); typical field length 3,300ft (1,000m); combat radius (hi-lo-hi, 4,410lb/2,000kg external weapons and two tanks) 345 miles (556km).
Armament: Large 30mm twin-barrel gun in forward fuselage; eight underwing pylons for varied ordnance loads up to 9,920lb (4,500kg) including ASMs, rockets and incendiary, chemical cluster and anti-personnel bombs; small outboard pylons for self-defence K-13A or R-60 AAMs.
History: First flight 1976; service entry 1981

Some of the latest Soviet combat aircraft to enter service seem to have been inspired by US prototypes, and in this case the similarity to the Northrop A-9A (losing finalist in the USAF AX competition) is obvious. Winner of the AX was the Fairchild A-10A, and by comparison with this the Su-25 is rather smaller and lighter, but it has roughly similar power and is faster. The main purpose is the same: attacks on ground targets in close support of friendly ground forces, with particular capability to take out heavy armour, fortifications and similar well protected targets. The design is thus biased in favour of short field length, independence of ground services, good low-level manoeuvrability and a high degree of immunity to ground fire up to about 23mm calibre.

Since 1982 small numbers of Su-25s — which curiously have a fighter (odd-number) designation, despite having little pretension to air-combat capability — have seen much action against the Mujaheddin in Afghanistan, who have commented on its long flight endurance at low level. It has operated with heavy bombs, very large numbers (a theoretical maximum of 320) of rockets and a high-velocity gun, and has often collaborated with Mi-24 "Hind-D" helicopters in making carefully combined attacks on the same target.

In typically Soviet manner the Su-25 was planned as a basically simple and tough aircraft that would perform as predicted and give few problems. This being so, it is noteworthy that it took a long time to mature, and seven years after first flight it was stated in Washington that it had still not been committed to full production. By 1984, however, series production was building up at a plant at Tbilisi, Georgia. Over 500 had been delivered by late 1988.

The long-span wing has full-span slats (with a dogtooth discontinuity), double-slotted flaps and powered ailerons. On each tip is a flattened pod with an ECM antenna in the nose, retractable landing light underneath and airbrakes at the rear which open above and below. Avionics at present are austere, comprising a laser ranger and marked-target seeker and radar altimeter. A strike camera is in the nose, the usual RWR and IFF are installed, and in the top of the tailcone (which houses twin cruciform braking parachutes) is a chaff/flare dispenser.

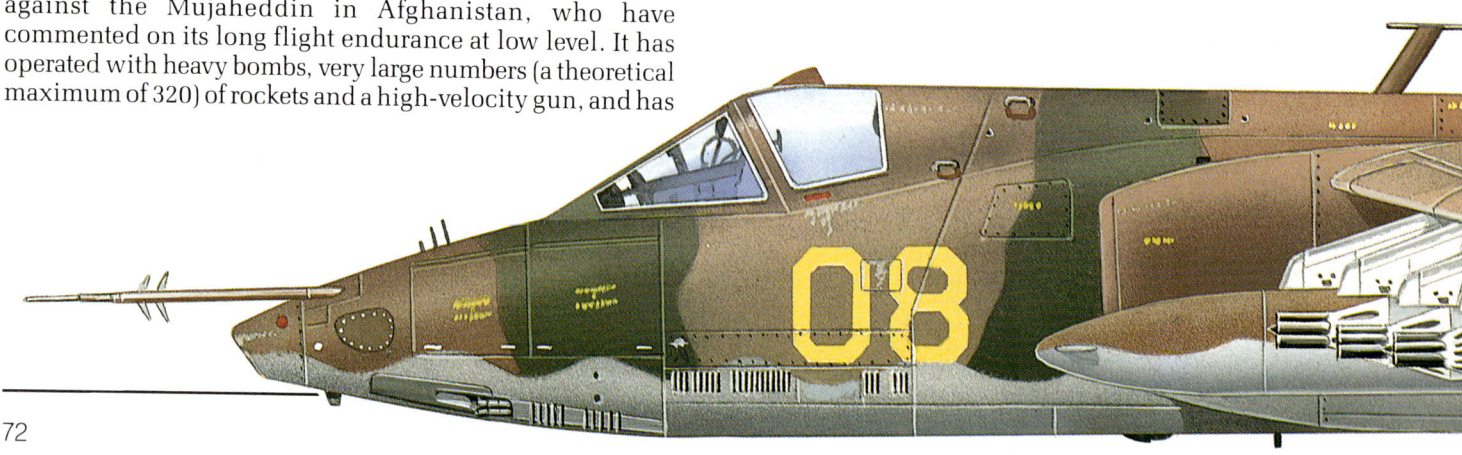

Sukhoi Su-25 ("Frogfoot")

Right: Upper view of an Su-25 loaded with rocket launchers and GP bombs. The powerful 30mm gun is inside the fuselage.

Above: The Su-25 has a nose-up "sit" in the sky. Equipment is extremely comprehensive, but not for all weather attack.

Left: The best photographs of the Su-25 to be available in the West were taken by Czech Václav Juki in 1985, showing Czech aircraft.

Below: Side elevation of an Su-25 of Soviet Frontal Aviation, many of which served in Afghanistan. Equipment is comprehensive.

73

MODERN ATTACK AIRCRAFT

Vought (LTV) A-7 Corsair II

Origin: Vought (now LTV) Corporation USA.
Engines: (D, H, K) one 14,250lb (6,465kg) thrust Allison TF41-1 turbofan; (E) one 15,000lb (6,804kg) TF41-2; (P) one 12,200lb (5,534kg) Pratt & Whitney TF30-408 turbofan.
Dimensions: Span 38ft 9in (11.8m); length (D) 46ft 1.5in (14.06m), (K) 48ft 11.5in (14.92m); height overall 16ft 0.9in (4.9m); wing area 375sq ft (34.83m).
Weights: Empty (D) 19,781lb (8,972kg), max (D) 42,000lb (19,050kg).
Performance: Max speed (D, clean, SL), 690mph (1,110km/h); (5,000ft/1,525m, with 12 Mk 82 bombs) 646mph (1,040km/h); tactical radius (unspecified) 715 miles (1,151km).
Armament: One 20mm M61A-1 gun with 1,000 rounds, and up to 15,000lb (6,804kg) of tactical weapons on eight hardpoints (two on fuselage each rated 500lb/227kg, two inboard wing pylons each 2,500lb/1,134kg, four outboard wing pylons each 3,500lb/1,587kg).
History: First flight (Navy A-7A) 27 September 1965, (D) 26 September 1968, (K) January 1981.

One of the most cost/effective attack aircraft ever built, the A-7 demonstrated the ability to carry such heavy loads and deliver them so accurately that in 1966 it was selected as a major USAF type, and 457 were delivered of the uprated A-7D version with the TF41 engine (derived from the Spey) and a new avionic suite providing for continuous solution of nav/attack problems for precision weapon delivery in all weather. This version also introduced the M61 gun and a flight-refuelling boom receptacle, previous Navy models (now retired from front-line units) having probes.

Like earlier models the D had landing gears retracting into the fuselage, a large door-type airbrake, folding wings and triplex power for the flight controls. The pylons on the cliff-like sides of the fuselage are usually used by Sidewinder self-defence AAMs. Most A-7 pilots have a high opinion of their air-combat capability, and rate of roll is good even with a heavy load of bombs.

In turn the USAF A-7D, 375 of which equip attack units of the Air National Guard, was the basis of the A-7E which is still a major type in the US Navy. A total of 596 of this type were delivered, of which 222 are equipped to carry the Texas Instruments FLIR pod on the inboard pylon on the right side, linked to a GEC raster-type HUD for improved night attack capability. Budget limitations have held actual supply of these pods to 110.

Newest of all the US variants is the two-seat A-7K, 42 of which have been distributed in pairs to 11 of the 13 ANG combat-ready A-7D units plus a further 16 to the 162nd Tactical Fighter Training Group at Tucson. A direct-view tube provides for Walleye and similar TV ASM guidance, and Pave Penny pods are carried for laser-guided stores, but even with "iron bombs" accuracy is under 10ft (3m).

Among European customers, Greece purchased 60 A-7Hs new from Vought, and these are virtually A-7Es. Portugal was eager to obtain more effective combat aircraft but had little money, and eventually selected 20 A-7As well-used by the US Navy. Before delivery these were completely refurbished by Vought to A-7P standard. The engine remains the TF30 but improved to P-408 standard, and the avionics have been brought up virtually to A-7E standard. Further examples, including some two-seat TA-7Ps, have since followed.

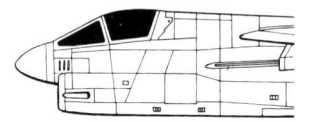

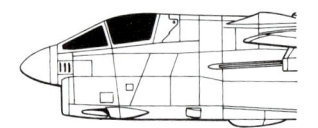

Above: Nose of an early A-7A as used by Portugal, with two Colt Mk.12 guns.

Above: Nose of A-7D, with an M61 cannon, FR receptacle and doppler blister.

Below: Side elevation of an A-7D as formerly used by the USAF's 23rd Tactical Fighter Wing at England AFB Louisiana.

Vought (LTV) A-7 Corsair II

Production of 1,545 A-7s was completed in 1983. Today LTV is upgrading 72 A-7Ds and eight A-7Ks with a FLIR, automatic terrain following and a GEC wide-angle HUD for low night attack missions. In 1987 the company received a USAF contract to rebuild two A-7Ds into YA-7Fs with a longer fuselage, more fuel, a common engine bay for the very powerful F100-PW-220 or F110-GE-100 afterburning engines, many airframe improvements and completely new avionics and systems. At the cost of much greater IR signature the rebuilt aircraft will have rather higher performance and should offer many other benefits. If selected for production up to 337 ANG A-7Ds could be rebuilt as A-7 Plus aircraft.

Above: Navy A-7A and A-7E Corsairs used a retractable in-flight refuelling probe.

Above: A bomb-laden A-7E of VA-147 formates with an A-6A while en route to a target during the Vietnam War.

Left: Underside view of the 23rd TFW A-7D, showing the weapon load of "slick" and retarded bombs and AIM-9Ls.

MODERN ATTACK AIRCRAFT

XAC H-7 (B-7)

The first modern multirole combat aircraft to be designed in the People's Republic — as distinct from being modified from a Soviet original — this impressive new twin-jet was designed at the vast aviation production complex at Xian (Yin Liang) to succeed the Chinese H-6 version of the Tu-16 "Badger". In the mid-1970s, the Chinese government obtained a licence to build the Spey 202, as used in the RAF Phantom FGR.2. Two engines were built and these sailed through their type tests in Britain. Then, nothing was heard for ten years until the prototype H-7 was rolled out in August 1988. It can be called the B-7 in Westernized form.

Little is known of this aircraft beyond what can be deduced from the model displayed at Farnborough in September 1988. So far as is known, no photographs were released of the first flight, which (if other modern aircraft are any guide) may have been delayed.

It was announced that the prototypes are fitted with main radar and terrain-following radar and various other avionics items "of Chinese design and manufacture". Indeed,

Origin: The Xian Aircraft Company, People's Republic of China.
Engines: (prototypes) two Rolls-Royce Spey 202 augmented turbofans, made at Xian under licence, each with maximum rating of 20,515lb (9306kg); (production version) expected to be the Chinese WS-6 engine in the 27,500lb (12,474kg) class.
Dimensions: Span approximately 41ft 6in (12.65m); length (excluding probe) approximately 61ft (18.6m); height, approximately 20ft (6.09m); wing area, approximately 400 sq ft (37.4m²).
Weights: Not released, but empty, in the region of 33,000lb (15,000kg); maximum loaded figure is probably about 66,000lb (30,000kg).
Performance: Maximum speed (clean, high altitude) about Mach 1.8, 1,190mph (1915km/h); maximum speed at sea level with weapon load, probably about 700mph (1127km/h); other performance probably somewhat similar to F-4 Phantom II.
Armament: One Type 23-3 twin-barrel gun under forward fuselage (exact form of installation not known as this book went to press); four wing pylons, shown on model with C-801 anti-ship missiles inboard and drop tanks outboard; self-defence PL-5B air-to-air missiles on tip rails. At the Farnborough air show, it was stated that the production version of the H-7 would have additional stores attachment points permitting the carriage of more weaponry.
History: First flight due November 1988; service with PLA Air Force due in 1993-94.

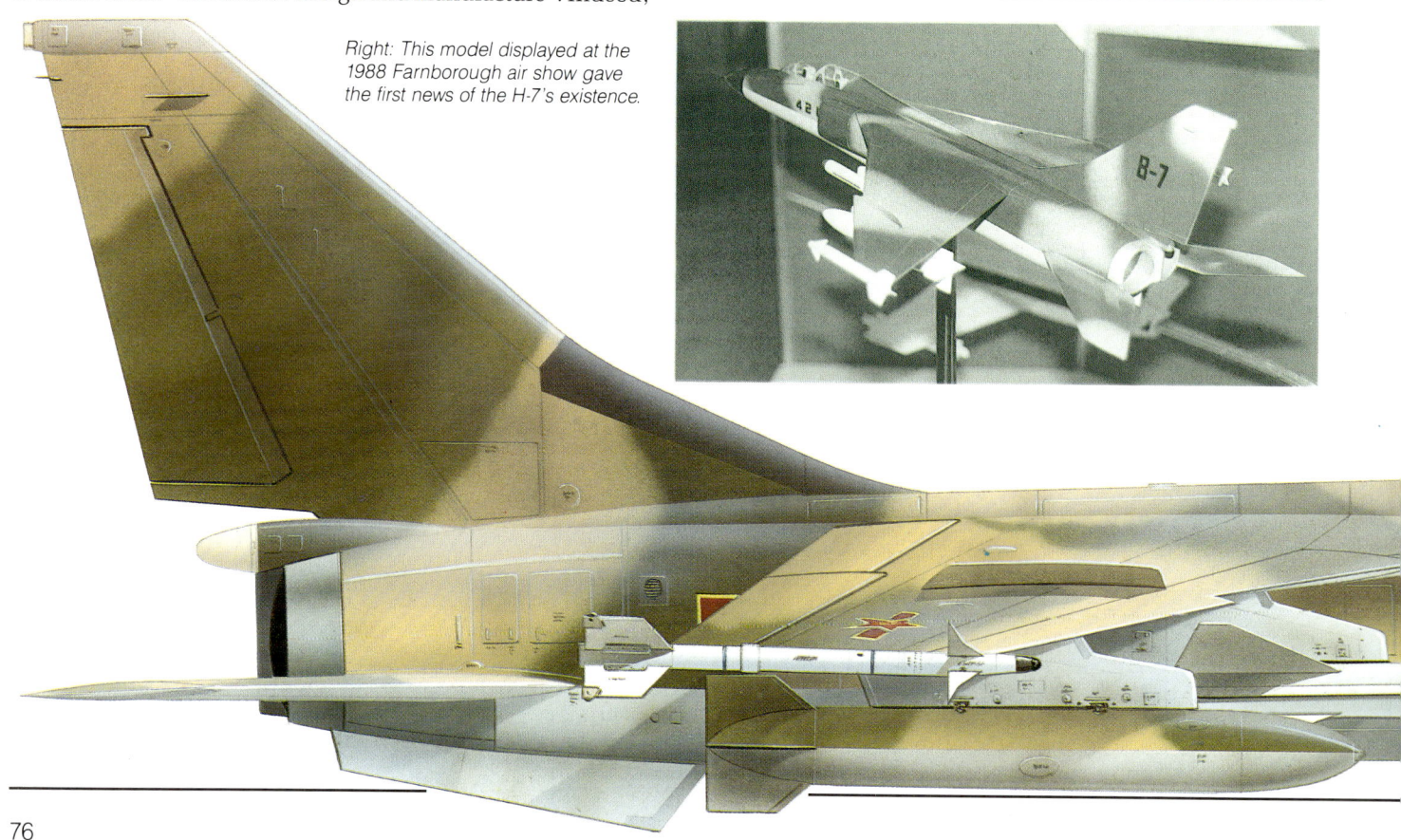

Right: This model displayed at the 1988 Farnborough air show gave the first news of the H-7's existence.